Beyond the Average Divorce

David H. Demo
University of North Carolina at Greensboro

Mark A. Fine
University of Missouri at Columbia

SAGE

Los Angeles | London | New Delhi
Singapore | Washington DC

For information:

SAGE Publications, Inc.
2455 Teller Road
Thousand Oaks,
  California 91320
E-mail: order@sagepub.com

SAGE Publications India Pvt. Ltd.
B 1/I 1 Mohan Cooperative
  Industrial Area
Mathura Road, New Delhi 110 044
India

SAGE Publications Ltd.
1 Oliver's Yard
55 City Road
London, EC1Y 1SP
United Kingdom

SAGE Publications Asia-Pacific Pte. Ltd.
33 Pekin Street #02-01
Far East Square
Singapore 048763

Printed in the United States of America.

Library of Congress Cataloging-in-Publication Data

Demo, David H.
Beyond the average divorce/David H. Demo, Mark A. Fine.
    p. cm.
Includes bibliographical references and index.
ISBN 978-1-4129-2685-0 (pbk. : acid-free paper)
    1. Divorce—United States. 2. Divorce—Research—United States. I. Fine, Mark A. II. Title.

HQ834.D46 2009
306.890973—dc22   2008049620

This book is printed on acid-free paper.

09   10   11   12   13   10   9   8   7   6   5   4   3   2   1

Acquisitions Editor:	Kassie Graves
Editorial Assistant:	Veronica Novak
Production Editor:	Karen Wiley
Copy Editor:	Renee Willers
Typesetter:	C&M Digitals (P) Ltd.
Proofreader:	Scott Oney
Indexer:	Jeanne Busemeyer
Cover Designer:	Candice Harman
Marketing Manager:	Carmel Schrire

Beyond
the Average
Divorce

Contents

Acknowledgments

This book represents the culmination of 2 decades of research that we have conducted on families' experience of divorce. We thank all of the families that participated in our studies and in the other studies described throughout this book. We owe a special debt of gratitude to the people responsible for starting and steering this project: David Klein, who recommended this project to the editorial group at SAGE; Jim Brace-Thompson, who served as our editor and offered valuable encouragement and direction in the early phases of this project; Kassie Graves, who provided steady support and guidance through the review process and the completion of the final manuscript; and the reviewers who carefully read earlier drafts of chapters and prepared detailed comments and suggestions. We also extend enormous thanks to Steve Duck, whose expertise we sought for Chapter 6, and to Stephanie Rollie, who delivered an excellent chapter under a difficult set of circumstances. The book was also greatly facilitated by a research leave to the first author from the University of North Carolina at Greensboro.

Like our other projects, this has been a labor of love. The collaboration was inspired by a lifelong friendship, and in many ways, working together with a close friend has been the most enjoyable and fulfilling part of this experience. Along the way, notably when writing slowed and other responsibilities distracted us, numerous friends, colleagues, and loved ones provided timely advice, thoughtful and constructive suggestions, and generous support. For their love, patience, and humor along the way, we thank our children who lived with us during the writing of this book, Brian Demo, Julia Fine, and Kenyon and Keaton Olson Fine, and our partners, April Few and Loreen Olson.

1

Introduction

Variations in and Fluidity of Divorce Experiences and Outcomes

There is perhaps no more appropriate adjective to describe the divorce process than stressful. Few individuals who have been touched by divorce would express any doubt that the divorce process is stressful for family members. The degree and duration of the stress may vary within and across individuals and families, but even for those who benefit from divorce, the experience is characterized by multiple stressors. Many argue that it is the single most stressful life experience, even more stressful than other major stressors such as job change, unemployment, chronic illness, or widowhood (Braver, Shapiro, & Goodman, 2006; Dohrenwend & Dohrenwend, 1974).

Not only is the divorce process a stressful one, but it is a very common experience. Divorce is experienced by a substantial number of people in the United States and, in fact, in Western societies in general. Because it is not possible to know precisely which marriages will and which will not end in divorce, demographers have developed sophisticated approaches to estimating divorce rates. Most estimates by demographers suggest that approximately half of married individuals will eventually divorce their spouse (see Amato & Irving, 2006; Bramlett & Mosher, 2001). This well-known 50% rate is computed from the number of individuals who marry and divorce in a given year; however, because these figures are based on different groups of people, it has been argued that these estimates are inaccurate.

Kreider (cited in Hurley, 2005), a demographer for the U.S. Census, has suggested that estimates calculated in this manner are inflated and that the preferred method to determine the divorce rate is to calculate the percentage of people who have ever been married who later divorce. Based on this method, Kreider argues that the divorce rate has never exceeded 41% and has declined slightly in recent years (also see Amato & Irving, 2006). Further, Martin (cited in Hurley, 2005) determined that this drop is due to a decline in divorce among college graduates. The divorce rate in the first 10 years of marriage for college graduates married between 1990 and 1994 was 40% lower (16%) than the comparable rate for those married between 1975 and 1979 (27%). The divorce rate for non–college graduates has remained quite stable over the same time period.

With roughly 40% of first marriages ending in divorce, societal concern has focused primarily on the consequences for children. Kreider (2007), based on U.S. Census data, estimated that 1.1 million children (15 per 1,000 children) experienced the divorce of their parents in 2004. Obviously, a much larger number of children will experience the divorce of their parents at some time before they turn 18 years of age. Partly as a result of the relatively high divorce rate, but not solely because of it (a child may be born to a single parent, a child's biological parent may die), many children spend a considerable portion of their childhood in family arrangements other than living with their two biological parents. For example, 26% (19 million) lived with one parent, and 7.2% (5.3 million) lived with a biological parent and a stepparent in 2004 (Kreider, 2007). As we discuss in more detail in Chapter 4, there are important demographic variations in the frequency of divorce and living in different family types.

Our focus on divorce does not mean that it is the only way that couples dissolve their relationship. Divorce is only one way—a legal way—to terminate one's relationship; the spouses also may separate from one another indefinitely and retain their legal status as a married couple. Thus, divorced couples should be regarded as a subset of the larger population of couples whose relationships have dissolved. Further, the divorced subset is not randomly drawn from the population of dissolved relationships, as those who divorce, as opposed to those who stay married despite the dissolution of their relationship, would seem to be more likely to come from higher socioeconomic status backgrounds, enabling them to afford the legal costs associated with obtaining a divorce. This difference needs to be kept in mind as research pertaining to divorce is reviewed in subsequent chapters.

Another important aspect of the demography of divorce is based on what may seem like an obvious point: The discussion of divorce rates pertains only to those who have the legal option to marry—heterosexual couples. Couples that are not married, such as cohabiting heterosexual and gay and lesbian couples, obviously cannot divorce. However, their relationships can and sometimes do dissolve, although it is statistically harder to identify both the beginning and the end of nonmarital relationships. Attempts have been made to estimate dissolution rates for nonmarital relationships, particularly in countries that have legalized gay and lesbian relationships in the form of registered partnerships.

Although some countries (e.g., the Netherlands, Canada, Spain, and Belgium) have granted gay and lesbian partners the right to marry, others (e.g., Norway, Sweden, Denmark, and some U.S. states) have permitted only registered partnerships, which is a legal status similar, but not identical, to marriage. In addition to the fact that all Scandinavian countries have legalized gay and lesbian partnerships (Andersson, Noack, Seierstad, & Weedon-Fekjaer, 2006), these countries provide a methodological advantage for researchers by maintaining very detailed and complete records on marriages and divorces (the legal dissolution of a registered partnership is also known as a divorce). Thus, it is somewhat easier for demographers to generate accurate population estimates of various family-related phenomena in these countries than in the United States. Andersson et al. estimated that in Norway and Sweden, respectively, 13% and 20% of gay male partnerships and 21% and 30% of lesbian partnerships are likely to end in divorce within 6 years (Norway) or 5 years (Sweden) of partnership registration. These rates are higher than the 13% of heterosexual marriages that end in divorce within 5 years in Sweden, but not higher than divorce rates in the United States (Andersson, 2002).

In the United States, dissolution rates for gay and lesbian relationships have been computed from the samples employed in several studies, but not from the population as a whole. Kurdek (1992) found a dissolution rate of 19% among lesbian and gay cohabiting couples over a 4-year period, while Gartrell et al. (2000) found that 31% of cohabiting lesbian couples with children had separated by the time their children reached the age of 5. These rates provide useful descriptive information, but are not very helpful from a comparative perspective because it is problematic to compare dissolution rates from nonrandom samples to the more representative data for heterosexual couples.

As is appropriate for a process that occurs as frequently as divorce, research has extensively examined the effects that divorce has on family members, particularly in terms of how family members who have experienced divorce compare with those who have not experienced divorce. Such comparisons have provided a wealth of useful information, and much of this knowledge base will be reviewed in subsequent chapters in this book. However, a central theme in this book is that these comparisons of group averages (means) often mask variations in how individuals experience the process of divorce. Students of statistics know that measures of central tendency provide an overall picture of the average score of a particular group, but they do not provide any information relative to variations in scores within the group. Thus, our focus in this book is primarily on these variations, and mean differences between groups are relegated to the contextual background.

※ PURPOSE AND GOALS OF THIS BOOK

Given the tremendous diversity and variation in processes, experiences, and outcomes that will be briefly introduced later in this chapter and described in more detail in subsequent chapters, our primary purpose in writing this book is to present a view of divorce that focuses on variations in experiences and changes over time. To provide a foundation for these emphases, in this chapter, we will describe two themes of the divorce process that have not received adequate attention in previous research and theory and that will be emphasized throughout this book: 1) variations in experiences and outcomes and 2) fluidity and change.

Variations in experiences and outcomes related to divorce. The first theme is related to the point made earlier that previous research has tended to emphasize differences in group means, such as the average difference between children of divorce and children from first-marriage families, on such adjustment indicators as school performance, behavior problems, and emotional adjustment. Mean group differences are important to examine, and they have provided a vast amount of valuable information. What is missing from this emphasis, however, is attention to the variability within each group in how children and parents react to divorce. Thus, our first theme is the considerable variability that characterizes the experiences and outcomes of those who have experienced divorce.

By experiences, we are referring to how individuals interpret the divorce-related events in their lives, how they make sense of these events, and how they place them in the context of their previous life history. Harvey and Fine (2004) asked college students whose parents divorced to tell a story of their divorce-related experiences. The narrative stories that emerged showed that there was substantial variability in the college students' accounts and that these stories fell roughly into four overlapping and not mutually exclusive categories: stories culminating in growth, stories of turmoil and despair, stories of father loss, and stories highlighting the complexity and nuanced nature of divorce experiences, such as chaos coexisting with resilience. Even within each of these categories, there was still some variability in the accounts of what transpired related to the students' parents' divorce.

Such variation in divorce-related experiences raises questions about at least two principal tenets of stage theories of divorce adjustment (see Chapter 6; Rollie & Duck, 2006)—that there is a high degree of uniformity in how individuals experience divorce and that well-adjusted individuals progress in a linear sequence through a series of defined and discontinuous stages. The poignant stories in the Harvey and Fine (2004) study show very clearly that young adults whose parents divorced share a number of experiences with each other, but that they also have many unique experiences as well. The accounts also show that progress, even in the best of situations, is not necessarily linear and that periods of growth and resilience are intertwined with, and sometimes concurrent with, periods of turmoil and difficulty.

In addition to considerable variability across individuals in divorce-related experiences, there is also variability with respect to divorce-related outcomes. By outcomes, we mean the tangible markers of how well individuals adjust to the stressors they have experienced and with which they are currently coping. There are several different dimensions of adjustment reflected in these outcomes, such as socioemotional, psychological, academic, behavioral, and socioeconomic. Although people who are well adjusted in one domain are often functioning well in other domains, individuals may function well in one or a few spheres, but not in others. For example, it is not uncommon for children to perform well in school (i.e., academic outcomes), but to experience low levels of self-esteem and high levels of depression and anxiety (i.e., psychological outcomes). For this reason, it is important to distinguish among these different outcome domains.

As an example of how researchers can (and sometimes have) examined variability in outcomes in different family types, Halpern-Meekin and Tach (2008) compared outcomes for adolescents in four different types of two-parent families—those born into a first-marriage two-parent family (typically referred to as intact families); those living with their biological parents who are in a remarriage and who are living with at least one stepsibling (shared children in blended families); those living with only one biological parent, a stepparent, and shared children to the remarried couple (stepchildren in blended families); and those living with one biological parent, a stepparent, and no half-siblings (stepchildren in stepfamilies).

For our purposes here, the first two groups are of interest (other findings from this study are reviewed in Chapter 8). Although adolescents in both of these groups were living with their biological parents, those who were shared children in blended families did not themselves experience parental divorce, but at least one of their parents was previously married and brought a child into the household from this previous relationship. Those in the blended family group fared worse in academic performance, delinquency, depression, and school detachment. Although neither group experienced parental divorce, this novel comparative study is especially relevant to our focus on within-group variability. In most research examining family structure, these two family types are aggregated together into two-parent or intact families, but Halpern-Meekin and Tach's (2008) investigation shows that there are important differences within the larger population of adolescents who are living with both of their biological parents. In this study, it is unclear why there were these outcome differences, but it seems quite likely that stresses stemming from the previous divorces of the parents in blended families (i.e., before the birth of the shared children), the presence of half-siblings, conflictual relations with the previous spouse(s), or merely the greater complexity inherent in blended families may have contributed to these differences.

A plethora of scholarly attention has been devoted to the outcomes of adults and especially children during and following divorce. We review these bodies of scholarly work later in the book, with separate chapters focusing on adult outcomes (Chapter 7) and children's outcomes (Chapter 8). Unlike other reviews, ours places relatively less emphasis on average (or mean) differences among groups, but highlights variability and change in how individuals adjust to the divorce experience. To the extent that the research evidence permits, we discuss how divorce-related outcomes are associated with processes occurring before, during, and after the divorce;

how adjustment depends on the diverse contexts in which the individuals find themselves; and the specific domains of adjustment that have been examined in divorce outcomes research.

Fluidity of family composition. There has been a strong tendency in previous work to treat divorce and other family structure changes in a static manner (i.e., either they happen or they do not; an individual either is in a single-parent family or is not), whereas the more complex reality (and more difficult problem to research) is that children and parents tend to experience a variety of changes in family composition over time. Thus, the second theme emphasizes the fluidity and change that are inherent in family members' experience of divorce and related compositional changes.

One of the most striking aspects of children's and parents' family circumstances is their *fluidity.* Fluidity refers to the frequency and rate of changes in family-related experiences and outcomes. In this chapter, we focus on the fluidity of family composition (Burton & Jayakody, 2001); fluidity in other divorce-related outcomes and experiences is addressed in subsequent chapters. Perhaps because of researchers' tendency to study family composition at only a single point in time, there has been a tendency to think that family composition is quite stable. And indeed, it is stable in some ways for the decreasing proportion of family members who grow up in a nondisrupted family and who experience no transitions in their marital or parenting statuses as adults. But for many or even most other children and adults, it is common to experience frequent changes in family composition. Wu and Martinson (1993) identified 187 unique sequences of living arrangement transitions among women under age 50 and found considerable variability among these women in the number of transitions experienced and the rapidity with which they occurred.

Research confirms that transitions in living arrangements are common for children as well. Wojtkiewicz (1992), based on analyses of the National Survey of Families and Households data set, showed that children in nonintact families at age 15 had typically lived in a combination of two-parent and single-parent family structures, suggesting that any one-time snapshot view of family structure can lead to misleading inferences regarding family environment. In addition, Wojtkiewicz found that children born to single mothers differed considerably in their experience of family structure from those who lived with both parents at birth. Children in the first group spent very little time living in two-parent families (i.e., with their biological mother and a stepfather), whereas those in the second group tended to spend approximately 50% of their childhoods in two-parent arrangements (i.e., in either a first-marriage or a remarried family).

In addition, because 30% of single parents cohabit with a partner or live in their parents' household, Bumpass and Raley (1995) argued that single-parent families need to be defined based on who is living in the home rather than on parents' marital status. Perhaps an unmarried parent who cohabits with a partner who plays a parental role should not be considered a single parent. Further, a sizable minority of children not only experience multiple transitions (see Chapter 9), but also experience the possibility of being separated from both biological parents (Teachman, 2002).

Not surprisingly, research has suggested that there are clear differences in outcomes for family members who live in different family compositions. For example, Oldehinkel, Ormel, Veenstra, DeWinter, and Verhulst (2008), in a prospective sample of Dutch adolescents, found that parental divorce was associated with higher levels of parent-reported depression for the sample as a whole. However, there were gender differences in how depression symptoms changed as the adolescents aged from 10 to 15 years. For boys, depressive symptoms decreased in magnitude for both the divorced and the nondivorced groups between the ages of 10 and 15. For girls, those who experienced parental divorce reported an increase in depressive symptoms over time, while those who did not experience divorce showed no significant change in depression. Thus, this study yielded gender differences in the depressogenic effects of divorce, as girls became increasingly vulnerable over time, whereas boys did not.

We will review this literature in more detail in Chapter 8, but the point here is that the fluidity of family composition is clearly related to significant variation in outcomes for family members. Such variation makes it misleading to draw simple generalizations regarding the effects that particular types of family composition (especially if assessed at only one point in time) have on family members. As discussed more below, we need new emphases, and ideally new models, to extend our understanding of how transitions in family composition affect the ebb and flow of long-term adjustment.

One particularly important type of transition occurs when children physically move from one residence to another. A recent meta-analysis (Bauserman, 2002) documented that joint physical or legal custody, compared with sole custody, has positive effects on children's family relationships, self-esteem, and emotional and behavioral adjustment. Even though joint custody appears to facilitate the ongoing involvement of both parents in children's lives, this benefit comes with at least a modest cost—the children may have to move back and forth between their parents' homes. This illustrates an important point relative to children of divorce: Even when they are placed in healthy environments, these contexts almost always involve change and stress for the children.

\\\ APPROACH

The approach that we take in this book is broad brushed, with particular attention devoted to variability in responses to divorce and the fluid nature of divorce. The book builds on recent theoretical models that guide the research literature on divorce and presents a new dynamic model of the divorce process. Our intent is for this book to extend our scholarly understanding of variability and fluidity in family experiences related to divorce. Of course, our focus on variability and fluidity is not new, but we place these dynamic dimensions in the foreground of scholarly attention in novel ways (see Chapter 2).

The book is divided into three parts. Part I contains three chapters devoted to the building blocks of scholarly inquiry—theoretical orientations, research methods, and context. Chapter 2 focuses on the theory building block and how it helps to guide our examination and advance our understanding of divorce. The key purpose of this chapter is to present our model (the divorce variation and fluidity model; DVFM) of how adjustment to divorce unfolds for adults and children; this model, as the reader will see, emphasizes our themes of variability and fluidity in the divorce process. We also describe how our model was informed by several theoretical perspectives that are commonly utilized in the study of divorce and its consequences. Chapter 3 focuses on the methodological building block by reviewing quantitative and qualitative research methodologies that have been used to study divorce. This chapter concludes with some new approaches that are necessary for studying divorce in a dynamic manner. Chapter 4 addresses yet another key building block— the societal context within which divorce unfolds. In this chapter, we consider changing values regarding marriage, divorce, and cohabitation; historical changes in divorce; the cross-cultural context; and the legal environment in which divorce occurs. Thus, Part I provides readers with the theoretical, methodological, and contextual tools necessary to understand the empirical evidence on the divorce process presented in the chapters in Part II and the implications for theory, research, practice, and policy described in Part III.

Part II contains five chapters describing variations in the divorce process and the multiple pathways characterizing the experience of divorce. Chapter 5 reviews the literature on variations in predisruption family environments and trajectories, with discussions of parent–child relations, marital relations, and children's and adults' adjustment during the period leading up to marital dissolution. We describe a range of factors associated with both declining marital satisfaction and an increased probability of divorce. Chapter 6, authored by Stephanie Rollie, focuses on variations in separation and uncoupling experiences, including discussion of common trajectories characterizing the separation process and the range of emotions that individuals experience. Chapter 7 discusses variations in and the fluidity of adults' adjustment to divorce, Chapter 8 examines the voluminous and controversial literature on variations in and the fluidity of children's and young adults' adjustment to parental divorce, and Chapter 9 analyzes children's and adults' experiences of multiple family transitions, such as experiencing multiple divorces, marriages, and transitions in and out of cohabitation. The latter chapter reviews literature related to how experiencing more than one family or parenting transition can affect family members' adjustment.

The final part of the book, Part III, consists of a single comprehensive chapter—Chapter 10—that provides guidance for future scholarly and applied work on divorce. This chapter considers implications for continued expansion of our theoretical model, suggestions for future research, recommendations for applied professionals (i.e., clinicians and parent educators who work with divorcing parents), and reflections on needed policy reforms. The implications for practice are directed at the individuals and families that educators and clinicians are ultimately trying to help, while the policy considerations are designed to make policies more sensitive and responsive to the needs and experiences of divorced adults and children.

PART I

Theoretical and
Methodological Tools for
Studying the Divorce Process

2

Conceptualizing Divorce Variation and Fluidity

Perhaps no aspect of family life is more widely misunderstood, stigmatized, and problematized than divorce. What does the divorce process feel like for most children and adults who experience it? Is it, as much of the popular culture leads us to believe, a uniformly wrenching psychological experience that wreaks havoc on everyone involved and causes devastating, often permanent emotional scars? Or is there substantial variation within and across families in the experience of and adjustment to divorce? How should researchers think about and study the divorce process?

In this chapter, we describe a theoretical model for understanding the divorce process and family members' postdivorce adjustment. Drawing on the voluminous empirical literature on divorce, as well as on a variety of established theories, we outline a process model that directs attention to variation and fluidity in children's and adults' adjustment to divorce. Our goal is to broaden understanding of how the divorce process unfolds; how it influences family dynamics in the years preceding, during, and following legal dissolution; and how family members cope and adjust. More specifically, our empirically based model has two central ideas: a) There is substantial variability in divorce experiences and outcomes, and b) the divorce process is characterized by fluidity and change.

\\\ CONCEPTUALIZING DIVORCE AND FAMILY FLUIDITY

It is tempting to think of divorce as an event that happens at some point in time in some families. For adults and children who experience divorce, however, there is no identifiable point in time that accurately encapsulates the divorce experience. A common theme throughout this book is that divorce is better understood as a process that unfolds over several years, a process that typically begins years before the legal divorce and extends for years following legal separation and dissolution. During the predivorce period, spouses' feelings toward one another gradually break down and a sense of apathy and unhappiness engulfs the relationship (Kayser & Rao, 2006). Conflicts between spouses may intensify, perhaps even becoming physically or emotionally abusive (DeMaris, 2000; Jacobson, Gottman, Gortner, Burns, & Shortt, 1996). Although there is great variation across families (see below), evidence indicates a common pattern whereby parenting practices become less consistent and less effective, parent–child relationships worsen, and conflicts between generations escalate (Amato & Booth, 1996; Hetherington & Kelly, 2002; Sun, 2001). Less often, but still too often, violence occurs between parents and children. In this climate, the emotional well-being of adults and children often deteriorates. Thus, an important point that we will develop further is that family relationships endure prolonged periods of stress, and family members exhibit declining levels of well-being in the years *prior* to physical separation and divorce (Cherlin et al., 1991; Sun, 2001; Sun & Li, 2002).

The process of marital dissolution unfolds in different ways in different families. Along the way, the spouses are faced with numerous decision points involving such issues as how much and when to disclose to friends and extended family members, whether and how to separate into two households, how to decide a variety of complex financial and legal matters, and, for parents, how to provide for the best interests of the children. As adults confront and negotiate these and other issues, potential pathways and timetables for future family transitions are set in motion. The divorce process thus generates additional fluidity in family composition by creating opportunities for a wide range of potential individual and family trajectories, notably including singlehood, cohabitation, single parenting, remarriage, stepfamily living arrangements, and redivorce.

⚅ CONCEPTUALIZING DIVORCE AND VARIATION IN ADJUSTMENT

Substantial evidence has accumulated from thousands of studies over the last several decades indicating that, for both children and adults, the divorce process is stressful and has adverse effects on well-being. Although there is some disagreement regarding the magnitude and duration of effects, as discussed further in Chapters 7 and 8, careful reviews and meta-analyses suggest a general pattern of consistent and modest detrimental effects on a range of outcomes for children and adults who have experienced the divorce process (for recent reviews, see Barber & Demo, 2006; Braver et al., 2006). In this chapter and throughout much of this book, we take as empirically established this general pattern, and we direct our attention to a different, largely neglected issue: How much *variation* is there in children's and adults' adjustment to divorce, and what are the most important factors associated with this variation? In the face of adversity, having experienced marital breakdown, disaffection, and dissolution, why do some adults rebound, feel relieved, and function quite well while others feel defeated or exhibit psychopathology? Similarly, having lived through years of stressful family relationships, the separation of their parents, reduced contact with one parent, diminished family resources, and a variety of other unpleasant or even painful personal experiences, why do some children and adolescents adjust successfully to parental divorce while others suffer long-term emotional and behavioral consequences? What proportion of children and adults who experience divorce are clinically maladjusted, and which factors are related to better or worse outcomes for family members?

In examining these questions, we simultaneously direct attention to the related issue of change over time, or *fluidity*. Specifically, a focus on fluidity leads to questions such as the following: How do family members fare emotionally and behaviorally in the years leading up to divorce? How does their well-being change during the actual separation and its aftermath? How are they functioning several years following divorce? Which factors account for faster emotional recoveries, and why are some children and adults still suffering long after the divorce?

To address these and other relevant questions, we describe a process model of adjustment to divorce. Although much of the existing research on divorce has not been explicitly driven by theory, a number of theoretical frameworks have implicitly (and sometimes, explicitly) guided work in the area, including the development of research questions, choice of research designs, identification of the sample, selection of measures, interpretations of the results, and the design of subsequent studies. In our model, we directly apply concepts and incorporate insights from six theoretical perspectives: a) the life-course perspective, b) family ecology, c) risk and resilience, d) divorce-stress-adjustment, e) account making, and g) feminist theory. We suggest a dynamic conceptualization that integrates ideas from each of these theories and that extends them by offering unique insights into the widely variable and highly fluid aspects of the divorce process.

Below, as we describe our model, we will depict how each of these perspectives has informed the model.

In Figure 2.1, we present the Divorce Variation and Fluidity Model (DVFM), an integrated model that outlines key processes influencing adult and child adjustment to divorce. The model is meant to be illustrative and heuristic rather than exhaustive, and our purpose is to demonstrate the highly dynamic nature of the divorce process and the complex set of marital, family, socioeconomic, and extrafamilial factors that affect how children and adults experience and respond to divorce. In particular, the model highlights the importance of marital and family relationship trajectories beginning in the predivorce years and evolving through the postdivorce period, individual and interpersonal skills and resources, socioeconomic changes accompanying and following divorce, reconfigurations in family structure over time, and alterations in family processes following divorce.

Explaining why some adults and children fare better than others following marital dissolution requires attention to three aspects of adjustment: a) average (mean) levels for the group as a whole, b) within-group variability, and c) individual change over time, or fluidity; these are indicated in the box at the far right side of the figure. The model also includes several sets of variables that research and theory have demonstrated to be important correlates of divorce adjustment. Below, we specify how each of these variables facilitates or inhibits postdivorce adjustment, and we hypothesize mechanisms through which each set of variables influences adult and child adjustment.

Sociohistorical Context

As illustrated in Figure 2.1, the divorce process unfolds within the broader sociocultural context. In the sections that follow, we briefly describe the major components of the sociocultural context. A more detailed discussion of contextual influences is presented in Chapter 4.

Divorce Variation and Fluidity Model

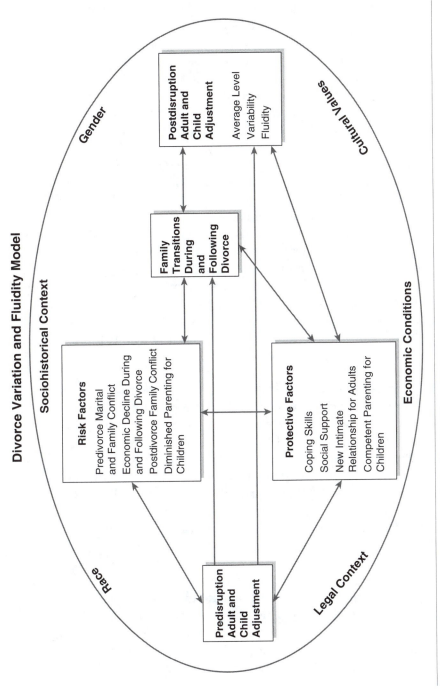

Figure 2.1 Divorce Variation and Fluidity Model

Support for the importance of considering the sociocultural context comes from a variety of well-established theoretical perspectives. The life-course perspective emphasizes dynamic processes of individual and family change over time. The lives of individual family members, the relationships they have with one another, and the pathways and transitions they experience are intertwined and socially organized (Elder, 1991, 1994). Sociohistorical events and circumstances (such as wars, terrorism, periods of economic growth and prosperity, or high unemployment and economic stagnation) generate or inhibit opportunities for individual and family development. Historical conditions, cultural values, and social roles create meanings for life experiences, family transitions, and the personal biography (Elder, 1977; Mills, 1959). For example, compared with experiencing divorce in a fault-based legal and societal context, experiencing marital disruption in a no-fault era and context is likely to generate very different social meanings and therefore different personal meanings and emotional responses. Further, individuals are active agents in their families and in the larger society, continuously making decisions and selecting roles and relationships in which they want to invest their resources. Thus, in many situations, individuals and families have the ability to activate resources to minimize misfortunes or even avert personal crises (Demo, Aquilino, & Fine, 2005; Hareven, 1987).

Sociohistorical influences on the divorce process are also suggested by family ecology and human ecology theories, which share the basic premise that families are embedded within an ecosystem. According to Bronfenbrenner's (1986, 1989) bioecological systems theory, human development and social interactions occur within nested ecosystems, two of which are the macrosystem, comprised of societal institutions, as well as cultural values and beliefs, and the chronosystem, which refers to the developmental history of the individual, to changes over time in the influence of different developmental contexts, and to sociocultural events that influence individual and family development. Bronfenbrenner (1979, 1986) stressed that the developing person is dynamic and that relationships and influences within each of the nested systems are reciprocal, such that individuals not only are influenced by different contexts and systems, but actively restructure their relationships and environments. This insight is particularly relevant to the study of divorce and family transitions, as individuals construct new lives, adapt to new living arrangements, and form new relationships and family structures. The placement of sociocultural context in the outermost circle of the DVFM was inspired by an ecological approach.

We posit that gender, race, and ethnicity are critical features of the sociohistorical context because of the profound ways they influence the experience of and meanings attached to divorce. Like marriage, parenthood, and other aspects of family life, divorce is experienced quite differently by women and men. Feminist perspectives emphasize the need to attend to gender as a central principle of social organization and social stratification and, by extension, as a central influence on family relationships (Osmond & Thorne, 1993). As others (Arendell, 1995; Emery, 1994) have demonstrated, Bernard's (1972) classic concept of his and her experiences of marriage can be adapted to describe men's and women's sharply contrasting experiences and perceptions of the divorce process. For example, wives tend to be more dissatisfied with marriage and see more problems in the marriage (Hetherington, 2003), they are more likely to have thoughts of divorce (Gager & Sanchez, 2003), they are more likely to file for divorce (Amato & Previti, 2003), they are more accepting of the end of their marriage, and, compared with their husbands, they have sharply contrasting experiences with grief, loss, and separation and have widely divergent interpretations of their children's feelings and needs (Emery, 1994; Walzer & Oles, 2003).

The aftermath of divorce also tends to be different for women than for men. Women typically bear the harshest economic consequences following divorce, and they are much more likely than men to have physical custody of children (Sayer, 2006). On the other hand, men are more likely to feel victimized by the custody system and other legal aspects of the divorce process (Arendell, 1995; Braver et al., 2006). Continuing family patterns that were well established prior to divorce, mothers invest substantially more time than fathers in parenting activities and responsibilities postdivorce (Demo & Cox, 2000). Men are more likely than women to remarry and to remarry sooner (Arendell, 1995), and, illustrating how race and ethnicity interact with gender, African American women and Hispanic women are even less likely than White women to remarry (Teachman, 2000).

Research and theory thus suggest the importance of being sensitive to gender in examining adjustment to divorce and attending to power differentials within romantic relationships. Further, a feminist framework emphasizes that family experiences, including divorce, are highly variable within gender. For example, as we discuss further in Chapter 7, Sayer

(2006) argues that a focus on averages masks significant variation in the financial consequences of divorce for men, and other studies provide evidence that although many nonresident fathers exhibit low levels of involvement with their children following divorce, other fathers are highly involved (King, Harris, & Heard, 2004). Thus, an important aspect of the DVFM is the need to consider both similarities and differences by gender in the experience of and adjustment to divorce.

Although empirical research on divorce has devoted less attention to race, there are strong reasons to view race as a potential moderating variable. For example, Orbuch and Brown (2006) illustrate that the context of divorce is much different for African Americans than for White Americans, with the former much more likely to face discrimination and other structural barriers that challenge marital and family relationships. African Americans are also more likely than White Americans to live in multigenerational and extended family arrangements, and they have larger and more active support systems. Orbuch and Brown argue that scholars interested in studying and understanding divorce need to consider race and ethnicity in all aspects of the research process.

Predisruption Adult and Child Adjustment

Within the larger sociocultural context, the DVFM begins at the far left (see Figure 2.1) with predisruption levels of adult and child adjustment. Consistent with the view that divorce is a process beginning years before legal dissolution, we use the term *predisruption* (rather than predivorce) to refer to experiences and to individual and family characteristics that predate separation and legal divorce. As suggested by a risk and resilience framework, predisruption adjustment is conceptualized as a predictor in our model because a higher level of functioning prior to family disruption should protect or buffer family members from stresses associated with divorce, while a lower level of functioning should make individuals more vulnerable to subsequent risks and adverse outcomes. A small but accumulating body of evidence indicates that children and adults who are better adjusted prior to divorce tend to be better adjusted following divorce (Hetherington & Kelly, 2002; Sun, 2001). Further, consistent with the life course and family ecology frameworks, we view individuals as active agents in constructing their relationships and life histories. According to this view, prior adjustment is expected to influence subsequent family relationships, dynamics, and processes, which, in turn, influence later adjustment.

Risk and Protective Factors

In the DVFM, predisruption levels of functioning are subsequently affected by two simultaneously occurring processes: *risk factors* that are stressful to individuals, couples, and families and *protective factors* that buffer those risks. Empirical evidence suggests that a risk and resilience perspective is particularly useful for understanding the wide variation characterizing family members' adjustment to experiences associated with family disruption and reformation (Hetherington & Kelly, 2002). Risk factors increase the likelihood of negative developmental outcomes, and *risk mechanisms* refer to personal characteristics or attributes of the stressor that make an individual vulnerable to the stressor (Rutter, 1994).

What are the risk factors associated with the divorce process? First, there are a number of predivorce stressors that increase the risk of adverse outcomes (see Figure 2.1). Prior to separation, marital processes such as marital unhappiness, tension, conflict, and violence (discussed at length in Chapters 5 and 6) are stressful and deleterious to the well-being of adults and children alike. Similarly, high levels of conflict and low levels of warmth and support in the parent–child relationship present risk factors for parents and children confronting the stresses of family disruption.

Other stressors during and following divorce include declining economic resources, lingering attachment to or continuing conflict with the ex-spouse, time-intensive responsibilities associated with sole parenting (primarily for mothers), or substantially reduced contact with children (primarily for fathers) (Amato, 2000). Personal characteristics that constitute risk factors for adults include problematic behavior (e.g., alcoholism), antisocial personality, impulsivity, and neuroticism (Hetherington & Kelly, 2002).

For children and adolescents whose parents are divorcing or who have divorced, evidence suggests that common risk factors include overt parental conflict (i.e., conflict that the children or adolescents directly observe) (Ahrons, 2004; Cummings, Goeke-Morey, & Papp, 2004; Hetherington, 1999; Simons & Associates, 1996), diminished parental monitoring and support after divorce (Demo & Acock, 1996a; Rodgers & Rose, 2002), and reduced contact with the nonresidential parent (Emery & Forehand, 1994; Hetherington, 1999; Kelly & Emery, 2003). Socioeconomic hardship is an additional stressor, straining family resources and negatively affecting parenting effectiveness and child well-being (McLanahan & Sandefur, 1994; Pong & Ju, 2000; Simons & Associates, 1996; Sun & Li, 2002, 2007).

We view risk factors as mediating processes that interact with protective factors to influence family members' adjustment to divorce (Demo et al. 2005; Emery & Forehand, 1994), as symbolized by the bidirectional arrow between risk factors and protective factors in Figure 2.1. This suggests that we need to simultaneously consider the types and levels of risk and protective factors influencing adjustment to divorce (Demo et al., 2005). We will discuss some of the methodological implications of this approach in Chapter 3.

Protective factors refer to personal traits, family resources, and family interactions that facilitate resilience, or that buffer the effects of risk. Research that has tracked adults for several years following divorce has identified a common set of protective factors among those who are better adjusted, including social maturity, autonomy, an internal locus of control, social support, and a new and satisfying intimate relationship (Hetherington & Kelly, 2002). Protective factors operating to reduce the risks of divorce for children include competent parenting by residential and nonresidential parents, diminished or low levels of conflict between parents following divorce, and supportive relationships with peers (Demo & Acock, 1996a; Hetherington, 1999; Kelly & Emery, 2003; Rodgers & Rose, 2002). Orbuch and Brown (2006) presented evidence that three strengths-based factors that protect African American families who have experienced divorce are extended family relationships and multigenerational households, ties to grandparents, and support systems consisting of church members and friends.

In the DVFM, protective factors are conceptualized as mediating processes that have the potential to offset risk factors. How well individual children and adults adjust to divorce is determined by the extent to which protective factors are present, including individual resources (e.g., coping skills), interpersonal resources (e.g., social support), and the definition and meaning attached to the divorce (e.g., perceptions of who initiated the divorce) (see Hopper, 1993, 2001; Wang & Amato, 2000). Amato (2000) argues that a divorce-stress-adjustment perspective recognizes that, for some children and adults, divorce represents a chronic strain resulting in long-term emotional and economic decline, whereas, for most, divorce is a relatively short-term crisis, after which individual functioning returns to predisruption levels.

〰 FAMILY TRANSITIONS DURING AND FOLLOWING DIVORCE

Life-course theory posits that studying transition experiences is essential to understanding life trajectories and developmental change (Elder, 1998). *Family transitions* are changes in family structure or household living arrangements, including adults moving into or out of the household to begin or terminate cohabiting, marital, or remarital relationships. We conceptualize family transitions that occur during the divorce process (including transitions prior to and following divorce) as moderating the impact of family disruption on individual adjustment. Adults establishing new romantic relationships may choose to remain single, often as single parents, or they may enter cohabiting arrangements. Many other adults remarry, some quickly, and many form stepfamilies. Each of these transitions, as well as the timing, duration, and quality of the relationships, influences how family members adjust to the earlier experience of divorce. In Chapter 9, we discuss adults' and children's experience of multiple changes in living arrangements.

Postdisruption Adult and Child Adjustment

A voluminous literature has examined how children fare in terms of behavioral, emotional, social, and academic adjustment in the years following parental divorce. A smaller but sizable literature has focused on the consequences of divorce for adults' socioemotional adjustment. We discuss three dimensions of adjustment throughout this book: a) average (mean) levels of adjustment, which have received by far the most empirical attention; b) within-group variability; and c) change over time, or fluidity. In Figure 2.1, we outline some of the influential factors that either facilitate or inhibit adults' and children's average adjustment levels, viewed in the aggregate. For example, higher levels of risk factors and lower levels of protective factors should theoretically be, and have been empirically, associated with lower levels of postdivorce adjustment. Although we view experiences following legal dissolution as part of the divorce process, for ease of presentation (as well as consistency with the empirical literature), we use the terms *postdisruption* and *postdivorce* interchangeably.

The importance of addressing the latter two dimensions, variability and fluidity, is suggested by the life-course perspective and its emphasis on heterogeneity. Within and across families, children develop at different rates, and they develop different skills, competencies, values, and coping strategies. Similarly, adults are quite diverse socially, cognitively, emotionally, and behaviorally. Differences by age, race and ethnicity, gender, socioeconomic status, sexual orientation, and other social structural variables introduce additional dimensions of heterogeneity that impact how family members adjust to divorce (Fine & Harvey, 2006b). As Bengtson and Allen (1993) illustrate, applying a life-course perspective with its sensitivity to heterogeneity provides an opportunity to expand our understanding of individuals and families beyond notions of "normal" development. Bengtson and Allen argue that "theories, conceptualizations, and empirical studies must consider not only modal or average trends in development over time, but also diversity across the range of patterns" (p. 472). Applied to the study of individuals' adjustment to divorce, this argument suggests the importance of extending the focus of analysis beyond measures of central tendency (e.g., means) to measures of variation (e.g., standard deviations).

Variability and fluidity in postdivorce adjustment are illustrated in research on account making (we discuss narrative approaches in Chapter 6). When a marriage dissolves, former spouses need to make sense of what happened. They need to process and reflect on the marriage, how it deteriorated, the role they played in the unraveling of the marriage, the role their former spouse played, and a host of other issues. Constructing a story, or an account, is necessary to achieve "peace of mind" and to move on with life, and an account of the events is needed for conversations with friends and family members (Harvey & Fine, 2006). Typically, there will be variations of the story for different audiences, including shorter, perhaps more socially polite versions, and longer, more detailed, perhaps more accusatory versions. Duck (2005; Rollie & Duck, 2006) refers to these stories as grave-dressing processes that allow each partner to mourn and memorialize the relationship, to portray oneself in a positive light and as a victim of betrayal, and to communicate an explanation, a self-justification, and a socially respected image. Such accounts serve varying purposes for different individuals, and former partners may have sharply contrasting accounts of the same events and experiences (Hopper, 1993, 2001), but accounts nevertheless play a crucial role in the process of coping with and adjusting to the stresses that accompany divorce (Harvey & Fine, 2006).

Consistent with life-course and ecological depictions of individuals actively shaping, and simultaneously being shaped by, their environment, account making emphasizes the creative, evolving, and socially constructed nature of divorce narratives. Accounts are critical in soliciting and mobilizing social support, thereby facilitating conversations that help the individual to work through unresolved aspects of the divorce and further refine his or her narratives. Harvey, Weber, and Orbuch (1990) developed a model for describing the stages that individuals experience in reacting to and recovering from a major loss such as divorce. Initial reactions typically involve shock, outcry, and denial. The individual then begins to develop an account, works through the reality of the situation and confides in others, completes the story, accepts it, and finally forms a new identity. Consistent with our focus on variability, Harvey et al. emphasize that the process unfolds in different ways, in different sequences, and on different timetables for different people. Further, they suggest that some people do not grieve major losses and that some people may not need to disclose their stories to cope effectively. This perspective thus suggests the importance of account making for the successful adjustment of most adults, but it also suggests wide variation in both the degree to which divorced individuals confide in others and the degree to which they benefit from such disclosures. An account-making approach also illustrates our second major theme—fluidity—by demonstrating that individuals' divorce-related meanings and narratives change in multiple ways over time.

The DVFM described in this chapter requires considerable empirical testing and opens the door for a wide range of research opportunities. In the next chapter, we discuss methodological tools and strategies for exploring the three elements of our model, namely mean levels, variation, and fluidity in divorce experiences and outcomes, with our focus on the latter two, relatively understudied and underemphasized, elements.

3

Research Methods for Studying Variation and Fluidity in Divorce

Our goal in this chapter is to provide an overview of research methods that are particularly suited to studying variability and fluidity in experiences, reactions, and adjustment to the process of divorce. We do not provide an exhaustive review of all research methods that might be appropriate for the study of divorce because there are numerous research methods textbooks and even some books focused on divorce (e.g., Emery, 1999) that provide such an overview. Rather, we tailor our discussion of methods to issues that are especially salient for our focus on variability and fluidity.

We begin this chapter by discussing the characteristics, advantages, and limitations of research methods that have been used to study divorce. Then, building on the limitations identified, we review some existing methods that can be used to study variation and fluidity in divorce experiences, as well as factors related to this variation. We suggest that studies need to be designed to ask new questions related to variation and fluidity, and we conclude with some implications for future research, including greater use of some already existing methodological approaches and the development of new methods and statistical procedures.

⫸ CHARACTERISTICS, ADVANTAGES, AND LIMITATIONS OF PREVAILING RESEARCH METHODS

Barber and Demo (2006) identified four distinct foci, or tiers, in research on children's adjustment to divorce. The first tier, which is characterized by research that compares the adjustment of children in divorced families with those in first-marriage families, comprises a large proportion of the literature. The next three tiers of research have been more sensitive to variations in and the fluidity of responses to divorce, but comprise a smaller proportion of the literature. The second tier of research examines processes that may explain why some children do well following divorce, while others do not. The third tier involves the study of variability within divorced families and over time. Finally, the fourth tier capitalizes on the knowledge and insights gained from the other three tiers of research and focuses on developing and testing interventions to improve the lives of children and parents experiencing a divorce.

Tier 1 research designs. The primary research design that has been used in Tier 1 research is a comparative group design in which levels of various dimensions of adjustment for children of divorce have been compared with those for children from first-marriage families. Many of these studies (e.g., Amato, Hetherington) were seminal in their impact and played a critical role in the development of our knowledge base regarding the effects that divorce has on family members. There is little question that these studies provided valuable descriptive information on reactions to divorce.

There are several noteworthy aspects of these studies that use a comparative research design. They can be framed in terms of limitations in the inferences that can be generated from their findings:

- They compare the various group means on children's adjustment dimensions. Thus, such studies test whether children, on average, do better or worse in some family structure groups than others.
- The very foundation of these group comparisons is nomothetic in the sense that the question of interest involves comparisons of groups in terms of the typical child in the respective groups. Thus, such studies basically indicate whether, for example, the typical child (defined by the mean score for the group) in a divorced family

has similar or different levels of self-esteem than does the typical child in a first-marriage family.

- Tier 1 research does not take advantage of the information provided by measures of variability on the various adjustment measures. Indeed, statistical procedures for comparing groups on a particular variable depend on the extent of variability within each group, but such information often is buried within the analyses or presented as a parenthesized column in a table providing descriptive statistics on the various measures.
- Tier 1 research compares groups all things being equal. In other words, when two groups are compared simply in terms of their mean scores on particular variables, the comparison does not take into account a multitude of other possible ways that the groups may differ from each other. In the divorce versus first-marriage comparison discussed above, no variables other than the independent variable (divorce vs. first marriage) and the dependent variable (e.g., child adjustment) are taken into account. This is a possible concern because the two groups may differ in meaningful ways other than on the dependent variables. In the divorce example, it is quite likely that the divorced sample has fewer socioeconomic resources than the first-marriage sample. And socioeconomic status has been shown to be strongly related to many dimensions of child adjustment, particularly academic performance. Thus, any simple comparison between divorced and first-marriage samples will not only be comparing on the basis of marital-family status (divorced vs. first marriage), but also between higher and lower socioeconomic statuses.

The astute reader may note at this point that group comparisons can be conducted controlling for some of these potentially confounding variables. Indeed, it would be preferable to compare groups after controlling for socioeconomic status and any other possible differences between groups to yield the most precise comparison possible between divorced and first-married groups. However, the use of covariates has limitations, including that there needs to be sufficient variability in the sample on the relevant covariates. If, for example, there are not a sufficient number of low socioeconomic status families in the first-marriage group or high socioeconomic status families in the divorce group, using socioeconomic status as a covariate will have minimal impact.

An additional concern with the use of covariates is that they create a pure comparison between groups, but these pure groups may not exist in the population. For example, if there were sufficient variability in socioeconomic status, we could compare divorced and first-marriage groups, controlling for socioeconomic status. Such a comparison provides a pure comparison between the two groups in the sense that, because the groups are equated on socioeconomic status, any differences between the means of the groups supposedly cannot be due to socioeconomic status. However, in actuality, divorced families have substantially lower socioeconomic resources than do first-marriage families. Having fewer socioeconomic resources may be an integral aspect of the divorce experience, and therefore, to control for this variable may create a divorced group that is quite different than it is in reality. Thus, the pure comparison has some scientific appeal, but creates a controlled contrast between groups that do not exist in reality.

An additional concern with Tier 1 designs is that they may confound family structure effects with family transitional effects. Typical family structure studies often consider family composition at a single point in time, such as first marriage, divorced-single parent, stepfamily, and sometimes never married groups. The problem, however, is that cross-sectional snapshot comparisons typically do not take into account transitions that have already taken place (e.g., previous marriages, divorces, or cohabiting relationships) or transitions that will occur in the future.

For example, participants in the divorced/single-parent group may include individuals with very different family experiences, varying on such dimensions as the number of previous divorces or the frequency of cohabiting relationships, whereas those in the stepfamily group may differ in terms of such variables as the number of previous marriages. Aggregating individuals with potentially widely differing family and relationship experiences into a single family structure group may mask potential differences that might have been found had these family transitions been controlled for.

Tier 2 research designs. Tier 2 studies have attempted to identify family processes that mediate or account for—in a statistical sense—the effects of family structure on children and adolescents. In essence, what these studies have attempted to do is to identify mechanisms within the family that may explain the differences in adjustment among children in different family structures. For example, numerous studies (see Barber & Demo, 2006) have found that reductions in financial resources available to the family partly explain why children in divorced families fare more poorly on several adjustment dimensions than do children in first-marriage families.

How do Tier 2 studies allow us to conclude that certain family processes explain why there are family structure effects on children? Typically, such studies begin by establishing that there are family structure effects on a particular adjustment domain. Then, the researchers assess whether the proposed family process variable is related to both the family structure that the children live in and the adjustment dimension of interest. If the family process variable is, indeed, related to both family structure and the outcome variable, it is possible to test whether the family process variable mediates the family structure–child outcome relationship. In this final step, the researcher assesses whether the relationship between family structure and child outcome is no longer statistically significant when the family process variable is considered. If so, then it can be inferred that that particular family process variable mediates the link between family structure and children's adjustment on that particular domain (Baron & Kenny, 1986). Parenthetically, we note that there are a number of statistical approaches that can test for mediating effects, including, but not limited to, analysis of covariance, hierarchical multiple regression, structural equation modeling, and hierarchical linear modeling.

The logic underlying the search for family process mediators is that if the family structure–child outcome link is no longer statistically present when one considers (or "controls for," in statistical terms) the mediating variable, then that may mean that it is *a* variable (not *the* variable; see below) that explains why the family structure–child outcome link exists. In other words, if we expanded our view to include the mediating variable, there would no longer be family structure differences in children's adjustment on that particular variable.

Several examples may help to illustrate this point. McLanahan and Sandefur (1994) studied whether family processes, particularly parenting behaviors and beliefs, mediated the relations between family structure (single parent vs. first-marriage families) and children's outcomes. They found that parental involvement, supervision, and aspirations reduced the differences between children in single-parent and first-marriage families; in particular, parenting behaviors were responsible for 50% of the differences between the two groups in school drop-out rates and 20% of the differences in early childbearing rates. Thus, McLanahan and Sandefur showed that one plausible, and empirically supported, explanation for why these two groups of children differ in drop-out and childbearing rates is that the parents in first-marriage families are more involved, supervise their children more closely, and have higher aspirations for their children than do single parents. In this case, we can state that these parenting processes partially mediate the relation between family structure and children's outcomes because the family structure differences still remained significant after considering the mediating variables, but the differences were considerably smaller.

As a second example, consider a study conducted by Kurdek, Fine, and Sinclair (1994). These researchers asked whether parenting behaviors mediate the relation between family structure and young adolescents' grades, physical health, drug use, self-esteem, and self-mastery. Interestingly, unlike the McLanahan and Sandefur study, Kurdek et al. found that there were still family structure differences of similar magnitude on these adjustment dimensions (with young adolescents in first-marriage families faring better than those in other family structures) even after considering the influence of how permissive, authoritative, and authoritarian the parents were. In other words, even after taking parenting into account, young adolescents in first-marriage families still functioned better than did those in other family structures. It is noteworthy that the parenting variables had a stronger impact on adolescent adjustment than did family structure, but both sets of variables made independent and reliable contributions to adolescent adjustment, meaning that the effects of parenting on adolescents were stronger in magnitude than was the effect of family structure.

As a final example, let us revisit financial resources as a mediating variable. Emery (1999) demonstrated that the magnitude of the difference in the adjustment of children in first-marriage families and those in single-parent families was reduced substantially, and sometimes to nonsignificant levels, after considering family income. In academic outcomes, for example, the advantage of children in first-marriage families was reduced by 50%. This suggests that a decrease in economic resources may be one of the mechanisms that causes children from divorced families to fare somewhat more poorly in school than their counterparts in first-marriage families.

Strengths of these designs include that they look beyond the surface toward the actual mechanisms that account for why family structure is related to children's outcomes. By itself, family structure per se cannot directly affect children's development; it can only do so via some actual day-to-day mechanism, such as family processes or family resources. For example, the legal event of divorce, by itself, cannot be causally responsible for child outcomes. However, it can be indirectly responsible, by affecting family relevant processes (like those described above) that, in turn, affect children. Thus, Tier 2 designs represent admirable attempts to identify and test these possible mechanisms.

Weaknesses of Tier 2 studies include, first, that the designs do not literally allow one to infer that the mediating variable causes there to be a link between family structure and the child outcome variable. The designs only test whether the mediating variable may explain this link. If the mediating mechanism is not statistically supported, then the family resource or family process variable could not explain the family structure–child outcome link, unless there is some methodological flaw (e.g., a weak measure that does not assess the construct that it purports to) that has led to the lack of a significant mediating effect. If the mediating mechanism is supported, that does not allow one to conclusively prove that that particular variable causes the observed link, but rather such a finding indicates that the data are consistent with that explanation. There may be other plausible explanations that could also be identified in other studies.

This limitation is why it was important that we indicated above that the analysis seeks to identify *a* mediator as opposed to *the* mediator. Mediational analyses seek to find variables that may account for why there are family structure differences in some child, parent, or family outcomes. The search for mediators is based on theory or previous research findings. However, the finding that a particular variable serves as a mediator does not mean that that variable and only that variable explains why there are family structure differences in the outcomes of interest. The findings indicate that the data are consistent with the notion that the variable of interest mediates the link between family structure and the outcomes, but the findings do not tell us that the chosen mediator is the only one that could do so. Other analyses may very well establish that additional variables, perhaps many of them, could also mediate the family structure–outcome relation. Thus, mediational analyses always need to be interpreted with an understanding that the results support an explanation, but that there are a number of other explanations that also could be supported. For example, the finding that a loss of financial resources mediates the relation between family structure and children's academic outcomes does not rule out the possibility that there are also other variables, such as unresponsive parenting and lingering postdisruption parental conflict, that could also serve as mediators. In fact, subsequent analyses could establish that other variables serve as even more potent mediators than the ones tested in an earlier study. Consequently, the search for causal explanations of divorce effects requires repeated and frequent study of the topic over an extended period of time, with a range of methods, samples, data collection approaches, proposed mediators, and measures.

In fact, this caveat regarding causal inference is an important issue to keep in mind with any model-testing statistical approach. Whether the analytic strategy is multiple regression, structural equation modeling, or hierarchical linear modeling, the ability to draw causal inferences from the results of a study (e.g., a decline in financial resources explains why divorce is associated with poorer child outcomes), which is also known as *internal validity*, depends on the research design, not on the manner in which the data are analyzed. In terms of establishing cause-and-effect relations, the strongest design is an experimental one, which, unfortunately, is typically impossible to implement in the study of naturally occurring family events such as divorce. Longitudinal designs that enable one to predict later outcomes from earlier events are stronger in this sense than are cross-sectional designs that only gather data at a single point in time.

A second weakness of Tier 2 research is that it is still based on group aggregates or composites in the sense that the results test whether, in general, a particular family process or family resource variable mediates the link between family structure and children's outcomes for the sample as a whole. In other words, the results need to be interpreted in terms of a typical or average child, and not necessarily for each and every child in the sample. For some children, for example, a decrease in family income may not be related to their postdisruption outcomes, even though the results for the sample as a whole suggest that family income is a significant mediator. Thus, assessing variability among children (or among parents or families, depending on the population of interest) is peripheral to the focus on identifying group trends. In fairness, the use of growth curve analyses (a version of hierarchical linear modeling that is discussed in more detail below) can examine individual differences in the rate and nature of change over time, but very few studies in the divorce area have used these advanced analytic strategies, which require a minimum of three data collection points.

Tier 3 research designs. Tier 3 research is inspired by the observation that some children fare quite well following divorce, whereas other children experience behavioral, academic, or psychological problems. Thus, the third tier of divorce research focuses on the extensive variability that exists in divorced families and the fluidity characterizing family members' adjustment over time. Rather than examining how children and parents from divorced families on average differ from other family structure groups, many of these studies have examined only divorced families (i.e., within-group designs) and have made increasing use of longitudinal designs that assess fluidity by testing participants on at least two occasions over time.

Barber and Demo (2006) indicated that not only do Tier 3 research designs examine the wide range in children's (and parents') levels of adjustment following divorce and how children's (and parents') well-being changes over time from preseparation to many years following separation and divorce, but also they address two other key issues. First, such studies have identified preseparation child, parent, and family factors that predict subsequent postdisruption adjustment. Note that the pursuit of family-related predictors of later postdisruption outcomes would utilize a sample of only divorced individuals (a within-group analysis) and that one would not need to include comparison groups of individuals from other family structures. These studies are perhaps the most direct way to empirically address the issue of determining which children, parents, and families do well following divorce and which ones do not.

Second, some Tier 3 studies have examined how children and adults adjust when they experience multiple family structure transitions. These studies address an often overlooked observation: Many children and adults experience more than one divorce (or other types of parenting and family transitions), and the effects of divorce may vary depending on the frequency of such transitions. The general pattern of findings from the few studies in this area (see Chapter 9) is that children and adults who experience more than one major transition (such as multiple divorces and remarriages) are much more likely to have adjustment problems than are children and adults who have experienced fewer (or no) family structure transitions.

Why are studies of the consequences of multiple parenting transitions categorized as Tier 3 studies? They fall within this category because they examine within-group differences (i.e., subgroups of children and adults within divorced families) in postdisruption outcomes and some of these studies have attempted to identify factors that predict differences in adjustment trajectories over time among individuals in these subgroups of divorced families. For example, studies have compared how children who have experienced one parenting transition (i.e., the divorce of their parents) fare over time in comparison with those who have experienced more than one parenting transition (e.g., a parental divorce and a subsequent parental remarriage). It should be noted that multiple parenting transitions studies do not maximally take advantage of variability within the different parenting transition groups, as they have tended to compare the average or typical levels of adjustment across the various transition groups and how these groups, in aggregate, differ in their adjustment trajectories over time.

Of the four tiers of research, the third tier is most compatible with the thrust of this book. Variability, in at least some studies, is the primary focus of such investigations, rather than mean differences between groups. Further, the longitudinal Tier 3 studies have obviously focused explicitly on variability in adjustment-related change over time. In addition, the focus of many of these studies has been on comparing different subgroups within the divorced population, which adds to our understanding of which family members fare better than others following divorce.

A final point of note regarding Tier 3 studies is that not all of them have been quantitative. There is a relatively small group of qualitative studies that have involved in-depth analyses of the experiences of family members who have undergone divorce and how family members interpret and frame their divorce-related experiences. For example, Harvey and Fine (2004) obtained detailed written descriptions of college students' memories of their predivorce and postdivorce experiences and, based on a qualitative thematic analysis of the more than 900 narratives they gathered, identified four general categories that were approximately equal in prominence: 1) those that emphasized negative themes (labeled as *despair*); 2) those that emphasized positive themes (labeled as *hope*); 3) those that emphasized missing a parent, particularly a father (labeled as *becoming fatherless*); and 4) those that emphasized family dysfunction and adaptation (labeled as *family chaos and resilience*). Many of the narratives could have been placed in more than one category, and most narratives described, at different times, both positive and negative experiences. These narratives provided support for the notions that there is extensive variability in students' divorce-related experiences and that there is considerable fluidity in how their reactions change over time.

Tier 4 research designs. Finally, Tier 4 research takes advantage of the gains from the first three tiers of research to develop and test interventions designed to facilitate the adjustment of family members going through divorce. The most common type of Tier 4 research is to use a particular set of findings and apply them to the development of specific interventions. A number of divorce-related interventions have been developed based on this general model: First, identify factors that are related to both positive and negative divorce-relevant outcomes, and, second, develop interventions designed to modify the frequency of these factors in growth-inducing ways. As one illustration, Tier 2 research has consistently shown that children adapt more effectively when their parents have minimal conflict after the divorce (see Barber & Demo, 2006). Thus, educational programs, including parent education classes for divorcing parents (Blaisure & Geasler, 2006), have been developed with the guiding principle that parents should minimize the frequency and intensity of their disputes, particularly in front of the children.

However, there is another way that Tier 4 studies can be conceptualized—a way that is far less frequent than the typical pattern noted earlier. Barber and Demo (2006) described how one can attempt to experimentally (through random assignment to groups) modify either individual factors (e.g., psychological or coping resources) or interpersonal factors (family processes) via structured interventions and then evaluate whether these interventions result in improved child, parent, or family adjustment. The logic is that if experimentally generated changes in some divorce-relevant factors lead to enhanced adjustment, then this provides further evidence supporting the notion that those particular factors are causally linked to improved divorce-related adjustment.

Some of the very few studies that can be placed into this category comprise natural experiments in the sense that they take advantage of programs or interventions that are already taking place in family members' communities. For example, parent education for divorcing parents has been mandated in a number of jurisdictions across the United States, and one could compare the adjustment of children and parents who have participated in such programs (because they are mandated to do so) with the adjustment of those who have not participated (because they are not mandated to do so or because such programs are not available to them). While these studies are not experiments in the strictest sense because participants were not randomly assigned to the parent education versus no parent education groups, these quasi-experiments (i.e., comparisons of two groups that may be different from each other in unknown ways) can yield valuable information about not only the intervention itself, but also the processes that are at the heart of the intervention (e.g., keeping children out of the middle of their parents' disputes).

Interventions are most effective when they are sensitive to individual differences among those who participate in the intervention. In other words, good clinical and educational practice requires that intervention activities be tailored to the particular circumstances of the participants. This is most readily apparent in clinical practice when a thorough assessment of the client's presenting problems leads to a treatment plan that is tailored to the individual's unique characteristics and circumstances. However, even educational interventions, such as classroom teaching and community group instruction (e.g., parenting education classes for divorcing parents) require some flexibility and modification to the particular needs and circumstances of the target group. The approaches that one would use to teach a group of high school juniors would be quite different from those that one would utilize to teach a group of parents from the community who have just filed for divorce.

Thus, because they need to have a sense of how their clients are functioning relative to others in similar circumstances, clinicians and educators are (or should be) particularly interested in information on the variability and fluidity in how children, parents, and families experience and respond to divorce. For example, a psychotherapist may be able to provide a more effective treatment plan for a divorcing parent if the therapist knows that the parent's depression score on a standardized depression measure is 2 standard deviations above the population mean and that the individual's score falls within the clinical range for serious depression.

EXISTING METHODS APPROPRIATE FOR STUDYING VARIABILITY IN DIVORCE-RELATED EXPERIENCES

At least three aspects of research methodology are relevant for fulfilling our call for greater attention to variability in divorce-related experiences: a) sampling considerations, b) data collection strategies, and c) data analysis. Below we describe the manner in which variability has been addressed in each aspect.

Sampling. Sampling refers to how one recruits and acquires participants for research studies. From a quantitative perspective, the goal of sampling is to acquire a representative sample that would allow one to generalize the findings to the population of interest (also known as *external validity*). The key distinction in quantitative approaches to sampling is between probability (e.g., random) and nonprobability (e.g., convenience) sampling. Random sampling allows one to generalize the results to the population from which participants were randomly selected, whereas nonprobability sampling can provide useful information, but makes it difficult to determine the population to which one can generalize the findings. In traditional approaches to sampling, there needs to be some variability in the characteristics of the sample so that there is some variability in their scores on the independent, dependent, and other variables used in the study. Greater variability increases the power of the analyses to detect statistically significant effects. For example, in a study examining how postdisruption parental conflict is related to the social functioning of children from divorced families, one would want to ensure sufficient variability in the social functioning (and the postdisruption parental conflict) scores so that significant relations could be found—if they exist in the population—between social functioning and postdisruption conflict. However, quantitative researchers do not typically feel that they need to deliberately seek out variability on specific study variables in their sampling strategies because their goal is to randomly obtain a sample that is representative of the larger population of interest. The assumption is that random sampling, or other variants of probability approaches, will typically generate sufficient levels of variability—an assumption that is usually warranted if sample sizes are sufficiently large.

Qualitatively, many sampling approaches use what are known as maximum variation strategies (Miles & Huberman, 1994), in which the researcher actively searches for extreme cases that do not fit the patterns and themes already developed. The notion is that one obtains a richer and more authentic picture or story of the participants' experiences if one actively seeks out diverse cases. For example, if the objective of the research was to obtain a rich portrayal of children's experiences when they are placed in the middle of their parents' disputes, one might actively recruit children from a range of ages, socioeconomic backgrounds, races-ethnicities, and so forth. Of course, the risk in maximum variation sampling is that the diversity in the sample will lead to such tremendous variation in responses that it is not possible to identify a coherent and integrative story describing the participants' experiences. Nevertheless, most qualitative researchers believe that the benefits that can accrue from maximum variation sampling typically far outweigh this risk.

Maximum variation also refers to deliberate attempts, in the midst of data collection and analysis, to identify and recruit cases that do not fit the patterns and themes already identified. If a prevailing theme in a study of nonresidential fathers is that they become progressively more distant from their children following the divorce, one might deliberately recruit nonresidential fathers who have become more involved with their children following divorce. The voices of these men may shed additional light on the experiences, desires, pre- and postdisruption trajectories, and behaviors of nonresidential fathers.

Data collection strategies. Data collection strategies are methods for gathering data from study participants. Quantitatively, typical approaches to gathering data in studies of divorce have included self-report questionnaires, behavioral observation, and structured interviews. All of these approaches yield numeric scores and, thus, are appropriate for a systematic examination of variability. Some newer data collection approaches include the use of diaries in which individuals are prompted (via the use of an electronic device or a personal computer) on a periodic basis to contemporaneously record their thoughts, feelings, and behaviors regarding a particular experience or situation. These approaches have the advantage of gathering data at the moment in which the thoughts, feelings, and behaviors occur, as opposed to retrospectively as is the case with more traditional methods such as self-report questionnaires. We are encouraged by the use of these new techniques and technologies because they will provide more reliable and valid information that will allow us to develop a more accurate and comprehensive understanding of variability in divorce-related experiences.

Qualitatively, nonnumeric data are collected via such strategies as interviews, observation, case studies, ethnographic approaches in which the researcher becomes either a member of or involved with the group being studied, and the collection of textual material from such sources as books, magazines, newspapers, television broadcasts, and so forth. A key underlying strategy of qualitative approaches is to work very hard to obtain the voices of the participants in addition to, or even instead of, the researchers' perspectives and impressions. Qualitative research considers the participants to be the experts on their own lives, and these approaches typically find a mechanism to tap into the unique way that each individual makes sense of and gives meaning to her or his experiences. Direct quotes from participants are typically used liberally to anchor the presentation of the data analytic results. We believe that the emphasis on participants' voices is an essential component of research on divorce that complements quantitative findings and enriches our understanding of divorce. Interview data and direct quotes from participants can help researchers make sense of the variation noted in quantitative research. In this sense, quantitative and qualitative approaches can be complementary and their integration has the potential to provide a richer understanding than can be achieved from either one alone.

Data analytic approaches. The most basic strategy for addressing variability with quantitative data is to ensure that measures of variability, such as standard deviations and variances, are computed and reported. In addition, one can statistically compare the levels of variability within two or more groups with an F test. Thus, one can determine whether one group has statistically greater variability in scores than another group, should that be of theoretical or empirical interest. For example, one could compare the variances (via squaring the standard deviations in each group) in children's academic competence scores between those who have experienced divorce and those who have not. To be sensitive to the importance of variability, most journals require that standard deviations, or some other indicator of dispersion, be reported along with means and other descriptive statistics.

As discussed further in Chapter 10, quantitative researchers can test whether certain variables are related to variability in a dependent variable. When one collects data at a single point in time, it needs to be noted that one cannot compute a variability score for a given individual (although such a score can be computed for how an individual's scores change over time, which we are referring to as fluidity). However, variability can characterize a group of scores. Thus, one could divide the sample into two or more groups depending on how much variability there is on the dependent variable (e.g., low, medium, and high variability groups). Then, one could compare scores on another variable—a predictor or independent variable— across groups to determine if the scores on the predictor variable differ significantly for the low, medium, and high variability groups. We could, for example, see if there is greater variability in children's behavior problem scores for those whose parents have been divorced more than once compared with those whose parents have divorced only once.

In terms of fluidity, there are a number of analytic approaches that assess changes over time. For example, *t* tests for a single sample and repeated-measures ANOVAs/MANOVAs (analyses of variance/multivariate analyses of variance) test whether there are statistically significant changes over time in a group's mean scores on one or a number of dependent variables. Regression analyses can determine whether a predictor variable assessed at a particular point in time (Time 1) is related to changes in scores on a dependent variable measured at both the initial and later time points (Time 1 and Time 2). In addition, as described in more detail below, some newer statistical approaches offer exciting opportunities to assess individual differences in rates of change over time and predictors of these different trajectories.

Qualitatively, most schools of data analysis involve some variant of verification procedures (Creswell, 1994; Miles & Huberman, 1994). Verification procedures are attempts to ensure that one's patterns and themes are consistent with (or authentic with) the experiences and the voices of the participants in the study. There are a large number of verification procedures, and several involve a purposeful search for cases that vary (sometimes extensively) from the typical cases. For example, *extreme cases* or *negative cases* are those that do not seem to fit the prevailing codes, patterns, or themes that have been generated. The challenge is to identify why the extreme or negative cases differ from the remaining ones and to determine whether they may necessitate a revision of one's thinking regarding codes, patterns, or themes (see George & Bennett, 2005). Some extreme or negative cases can be understood in such a way that there does not need to be a modification in the previously existing analytic structure, whereas others may suggest that the results need to be reconceptualized. For example, a particular divorced mother may supervise and monitor her children much more closely following the divorce than she did before the divorce; she may be an extreme or negative case in the sense that the prevailing pattern might be that parents supervise less closely following the divorce. How might this case help enrich researchers' understanding of the prevailing pattern? One possibility is that this particular mother believes that she must monitor her children more closely because she believes that the children's father is a particularly bad influence on them and that she has to compensate for his negative involvement by being more vigilant herself. Without an analysis of this particular divorced mother, our understanding would not be as authentic and rich.

Thus, extreme cases, unlike their counterpart in quantitative work (i.e., outliers), are not to be feared or avoided; rather, they are to be embraced because they enrich the work and bring new insights into the organizational structure of the data analysis. Thus, one way of conceptualizing the qualitative use of extreme cases is that there is an appreciation of variability among individuals in their experiences and that this variability is a catalyst for more refined and accurate attempts to understand their experience.

☒ RECENT INNOVATIONS FOR STUDYING VARIABILITY AND FLUIDITY

Quantitative approaches. In addition to the statistical approaches discussed earlier, there are a few recent innovations that are particularly useful for examining variability and fluidity. Each will be briefly described, and an example of each approach will be provided. The first, *structural equation modeling (SEM)*, is a model-testing approach that has several advantages that make it a preferred strategy over regression analysis in certain cases.

One advantage is that it allows for the creation of latent variables, which are theoretically derived constructs, consisting of combinations of a number of manifest or observed variables. For example, a latent construct of adjustment could be constructed from observed measures of school grades, social competence, and behavior problems. SEM empirically tests whether the manifest variables (in this case, school grades, social competence, and behavior problems) do, indeed, consistently tap the single latent construct (in this case, adjustment), which is referred to as the *measurement model*. Specifically, in this case, tapping a single latent construct means that school grades, social competence, and behavior problems are highly intercorrelated, most likely that high school grades would be related to high levels of social competence, and that both high school grades and high levels of social competence would be related to exhibiting few behavior problems.

A second, and related, advantage of SEM is that it takes into account measurement error, or the extent to which there is a lack of reliability in measurement, in scores on all variables included in the model. Regression analysis assumes that all variables are measured with perfect reliability, or with no measurement error. However, because of the inclusion of multiple manifest variables to assess a single latent construct, a lack of perfect reliability can be considered in the analyses, which allows for more accurate, realistic, and useful results. Thus, SEM is useful because it more sensitively takes into account the reliability of the measures and because it allows for the generation of theoretically derived and empirically validated latent constructs that permit the testing of specific research hypotheses.

Using SEM with data from a 17-year longitudinal study, Amato and Afifi (2006) examined a model that posited that parental divorce and marital conflict lead young adults to have stronger feelings of being caught between their parents, which, in turn, lead to lower subjective well-being and poorer quality parent–child relationships. The researchers found that parental divorce did not lead to stronger feelings of being caught between parents, but that marital conflict did. Further, feeling caught between parents was significantly related to these young adults' reporting that they have poorer quality relations with mothers and fathers and lower levels of subjective well-being. These results suggest that marital discord has a stronger effect on young adults' feelings of being caught between their parents than does divorce. The researchers' use of SEM allowed them to use multiple indicators (manifest variables) of parent–child relationship quality and subjective well-being, to take measurement error into account, and to empirically test whether the data were consistent with the proposed theoretical model. It is important to note that these data are supportive of the interpretations made above, but that the results do not rule out the possibility that there could be other plausible causal paths that also fit the data well.

A second recent statistical innovation is *hierarchical linear modeling (HLM)*. HLM allows researchers to take advantage of nested data. For example, suppose researchers are investigating the relation between students' perceptions of how much conflict there is in their families and their grades in school. They choose to study all 100 of the fourth graders in a school with four fourth-grade classrooms (25 students per classroom). The researchers could study all 100 students as a unit, but technically, this method violates an important assumption in the use of most parametric statistical methods—independence of observations. The concern is that the 25 students within each classroom interact with each other for many hours each and every school day; thus, their observations are not independent of each other. It is quite possible, and perhaps even quite likely, that there will be some similarities in how children respond to the various questionnaires or surveys because they interact together so often. HLM takes this into account by providing an estimate of the strength of the relation between perceived family conflict and school grades after controlling for the classroom that the children are in. In addition, HLM determines if there is a significant classroom effect on school grades and even more important, whether the relation between perceived family conflict and school grades differs depending on which classroom the student is in (i.e., whether classroom moderates the relation between perceived family conflict and school grades).

Hoffmann (2002) examined the relationship between family structure and adolescent drug usage. Although it has been established for some time that children from single-parent families engage in more acting-out behaviors, such as drug usage, than do children in first-marriage families, Hoffmann used hierarchical linear modeling to investigate the influence of community context on this relation. In particular, Hoffmann assessed whether adolescent drug use was affected by a number of community-level variables, such as the percentage of women-headed households, the unemployment rate, and the percentage of families below the poverty level, and then examined whether these community variables influenced the relation between family structure and drug usage. Because data from adolescents and families in a particular context are not independent of each other, it is important from a statistical standpoint to take this nesting into account. HLM allows the investigator to do exactly this, by estimating the community effects on drug usage, as well as considering whether community effects moderate the links between family structure and adolescent drug usage. In this study, Hoffmann found that drug usage was less frequent when the male unemployment rate was high and when the percentage of families in poverty was high. However, adolescents from non-first-marriage families still used drugs more frequently than adolescents in first-marriage families, even after taking community characteristics into account. This suggests that the effects of family structure on adolescent drug usage are independent of the communitywide effects on drug usage.

HLM is especially well suited to researchers examining variation in experiences with and reactions to divorce because it takes into account how individuals react in similar and different environmental contexts, whether such contexts include the community in which one lives, the school one attends, or some other contextual unit. Previous research, often using multiple regression analyses or path analyses, has often lumped together participants from similar contexts, which (perhaps incorrectly) assumes that the data from such individuals are independent of each other.

A particularly relevant variant of HLM is *growth curve analysis.* Growth curve analysis depends on longitudinal data with at least three observations per participant over time. In a typical first step, a growth trajectory on the dependent variable is determined for each participant in the study. Such a trajectory involves identifying the initial status (or score) of the individual on the dependent measure and then determining the linear and sometimes curvilinear rate of change on the dependent variable for that person. As a common second step, the researcher often examines whether individual-level variables, such as participants' gender, age, education, or any other individual difference characteristics, are related to either participants' initial status scores or their growth trajectories. Growth curve analysis, therefore, examines whether particular groups of individuals differ in either their initial levels on the dependent variable or in the rate of change over time. This approach embraces variability because, unlike such techniques as repeated measures ANOVAs, individual differences in growth trajectories are taken into consideration. Further, the emphasis on changes over time is fully consistent with our focus on fluidity.

Strohschein (2005) examined the extent to which parental divorce affected children's mental health trajectories. With a prospective Canadian sample of 4- to 7-year-old children living with two biological parents, Strohschein compared the mental health trajectories of two groups of children: those whose parents remained married throughout the 5 years of the study and those whose parents divorced during this time. Consistent with a trend discussed later in Chapter 8, even before marital disruption, children whose parents later divorced had higher levels of anxiety-depression and antisocial behavior than did children whose parents remained married. In terms of change over time, for the divorced group, there was an increase over time in anxiety-depression, but not in antisocial behavior. Despite the increase over time in anxiety-depression for the divorced group, the rate of change in anxiety-depression did not significantly differ between the divorced and continuously married groups. When a number of predivorce child and family characteristics were taken into account, the difference in initial levels of anxiety-depression between the divorced and continuously married groups was no longer significant, indicating that these variables mediated the relation between family structure group and initial levels of anxiety-depression.

Growth curve analysis is extremely sensitive to fluidity in responses to divorce by establishing both the initial status and the growth trajectory on the dependent variable. It can also be attentive to variability in the sense that different subgroups can be created to determine if there are differences in initial status or growth trajectories. For example, Strohschein (2005) found no support for the stress relief hypothesis that subsequent divorce in highly dysfunctional families (as compared with less dysfunctional families) leads to a reduction in children's anxiety-depression. Strohschein also examined whether the link between family structure and mental health outcomes differed by child gender and by the age of the child, and found that neither of these variables moderated the family structure–mental health trajectory relationship, suggesting that the relations between family structure and mental health outcomes were similar for boys and girls and for older and younger children.

Qualitative approaches. Qualitative advances in recent years fall in the nexus between methodology and theoretical perspective. One of these advances is a more fervent acceptance among qualitative researchers (and many quantitative scholars) of a postmodern perspective on theory and methods. The hallmark of a postmodern perspective is the notion that there is no single truth characterizing the social world and that there are many and varied truths depending on a host of contextual and cultural variables. In the divorce literature, there has been a growing recognition that there are both *his* and *her* divorces in the sense that each partner has a unique experience related to the divorce and each constructs a story or narrative describing his or her understanding of the events that occurred during the relationship, as it was dissolving, and after dissolution (Hopper, 2001; Rollie & Duck, 2006). Hopper's qualitative work (see Chapters 5 and 6) suggested that the partners' narratives can be quite different from each other, even though they are supposedly describing the same event, which suggests that each partner has a different version of reality with respect to the divorce process. This notion of multiple realities and experiences provides a new twist on variability, as it is not just that individuals vary along a single continuum of adjustment (e.g., postdisruption adjustment), but that different individuals may have quite varying views of what constitutes healthy adjustment and what transpired in their now-terminated marriages.

Another qualitative advance is the increased popularity of a critical approach to understanding social phenomena. The key premise of this approach is the notion that social relations, like those involved in the process of divorce, need to be understood in the context of power dynamics. Those in power tend to have more control over relationship-relevant outcomes and typically try to persuade their partners that their version of what happened is the most accurate or truthful one. Thus, those in power control not only relationship outcomes, but also the narratives that arise following relationship dissolution. A critical approach to scholarship is very consistent with a feminist approach, and the two are often, at least implicitly, used in combination with each other. To date, there have not been many critical analyses of reactions to divorce, with the notable exception of work that has examined structural, institutional, relationship, and legal reasons why men fare better socioeconomically following divorce than do women (Sayer, 2006; also see Arendell, 1995).

〰 CONCLUSIONS

Our analysis of research methods used in the study of divorce suggests that we already have in our methodological tool kit a number of strategies that lend themselves very nicely to extending our understanding of variability and fluidity in divorce-related experiences. There is not so much a need to develop new sampling, data collection, and data analytic strategies, but, rather, a need to implement already existing approaches in different and deliberate ways to more systematically collect and analyze information on variation and fluidity in reactions to divorce. Quantitative and qualitative approaches, ideally in synchrony but also on their own, can and should be used to place variability in divorce-related experiences in the foreground, rather than in the background, of divorce research.

4

Divorce and
Family Transitions
in Societal Context

D ivorce is a complex, multidimensional process that unfolds over many years. To understand why couples divorce and how divorce affects individuals and families, divorce needs to be considered in context, including the social, historical, cultural, and legal circumstances affecting individuals throughout the divorce process. In this chapter, we describe a range of important societal contexts surrounding divorce, including a) changing values regarding marriage, divorce, and cohabitation; b) historical changes in divorce; c) the cross-cultural context, including demographic variations in divorce rates among various subgroups; and d) the legal environment in which divorce occurs. Figure 2.1 visually depicts our Divorce Variation and Fluidity Model (DVFM); in this model, these contexts constitute the environment within which the divorce process unfolds. In this chapter, we elaborate on each of these contextual dimensions. We begin with the social context, which consists of values regarding family, marriage, divorce, and cohabitation.

CHANGING VALUES REGARDING FAMILY, MARRIAGE, DIVORCE, AND COHABITATION

Before discussing changes in values regarding marriage, divorce, and cohabitation, it is important to begin with the issue of how family should be defined. There are generally two types of definitions of family—objective and subjective. The prototypical example of the objective approach to defining family is the definition used by the U.S. Census Bureau (2008): "A family is a group of two or more persons related by birth, marriage, or adoption and residing together in a household" (p. 6).

The subjective definition is based on how people themselves view who is in and who is not in their family. This approach is exemplified by Allen, Fine, and Demo's (2000) definition of family—"two or more persons related by birth, marriage, adoption, or choice" (p. 1). The key difference between the two types of definition is the addition of choice to the subjective definition, which implies that a family consists of all of the individuals who any given person considers to be in his or her family, even if they are not related biologically or legally. This addition means that individuals may consider certain individuals to be family members because they feel particularly close or committed to them even if they are not biologically linked to them and are not married. Such individuals may include extremely close friends, people one respects a great deal, older or more experienced adults who one goes to for advice and guidance, and fictive kin who behave as if they were family members and who present themselves to others as kin.

Many quantitative researchers continue to use objective definitions of family because this approach permits them to relatively easily determine who is and who is not a member of any particular family. As we discussed in Chapter 3, quantitative researchers require standardization in how constructs are operationally defined and measured; the relative objectivity of definitions like the Census one is, thus, quite appealing. By contrast, the subjective definitional approach has the intuitive advantage of allowing individuals themselves to determine the boundaries around their family, thus respecting each person as the expert on his or her own family. Because of variation in who individuals will consider to be family members, it is more challenging with this approach to reach consensus or agreement on exactly which individuals are to be included in any given family group. This makes subjective definitions relatively unappealing to quantitative researchers, but quite attractive to many qualitative researchers.

What implications do definitions of family have for our understanding of divorce? First, the increased acceptance of the subjective definitional approach means that, unlike marriage or even cohabitation, it is not a routine or simple matter to determine who is in a romantic relationship and who is not. According to this approach, only the individuals themselves can determine if they are in a romantic relationship. Second, the subjective approach reminds us that many relationships that are not considered family relationships by the objective definition (e.g., by the U.S. Census) can be considered romantic and committed by the parties themselves. For example, a long-term committed cohabiting relationship would not meet the Census Bureau's definition of family, although it very likely would meet the subjective definition of a romantic relationship and possibly of a family that is very meaningful to both partners. Accordingly, even though such relationships are more difficult to define and identify than marriages, the dissolution of these relationships may elicit many of the same kinds of responses and reactions as does divorce.

These definitional and conceptual issues provide the background for other important aspects of the societal context surrounding divorce—societal views of marriage, divorce, and cohabitation. Each is considered below.

Societal views of marriage. Marriage appears to have retained its status as a highly desired institution (Cherlin, 2004). Almost 90% of Americans eventually marry (Goldstein & Kenney, 2001; Kreider & Fields, 2002), although this rate is modestly lower than those in previous years. Further, unlike previous generations when marriage rates were lower for more educated individuals, marriage rates are now higher for more educated men and women (Goldstein & Kenny).

In a survey of high school seniors that has been conducted annually since 1976, the percentage of young women who report that they expect that they will marry has remained at approximately 80%, the comparable percentage for young men has actually increased from 71% to 78%, and the percentages who indicated that having a good marriage and family life is extremely important to them has remained consistent at approximately 80% for women and 70% for men (Thornton & Young-DeMarco, 2001).

However, despite its popularity, Cherlin (2004) has suggested that marriage has become less institutionalized over time, by which he means that social norms governing marriage have become weaker. In Cherlin's view, two trends have contributed to this: 1) a change from institutional marriage to companionate marriage, and 2) a greater emphasis on marriage meeting individualistic and self-fulfillment needs, as opposed to fulfilling societal expectations of being a good spouse and a good parent. With the change to companionate marriages, spouses expect that their partners will be intimate companions, with meaningful communication, emotional satisfaction, cohesive interactions, and shared activities. Similarly, marriage is not only expected to fulfill emotional needs, but is now also expected to lead to spouses gaining individualistic rewards, such as personal growth, enjoyment and fun, and mutually beneficial intimate exchanges. As Cherlin has noted,

> Marriage is at once less dominant and more distinctive than it was. It has evolved from a marker of conformity to a marker of prestige. Marriage is a status one builds up to, often by living with a partner beforehand, by attaining steady employment or starting a career, by putting away some savings, and even by having children. Marriage's place in the life course used to come before those investments were made, but now it often comes afterward. It used to be the foundation of adult personal life; now it is sometimes the capstone. (2004, p. 855)

As a result of these changing expectations of the institution of marriage, married individuals have a different comparison level than those who married in earlier generations. Now, spouses expect that marriages will meet their intimate, personal, and companionate needs and are more likely to be dissatisfied when their marriage does not help them do so. This suggests that individuals may more readily and more quickly consider divorce as a realistic alternative to remaining in a conflictual and dissatisfying relationship than was true in the past. In the past, divorce often occurred when one partner engaged in some egregious behavior (as in fault-based divorce), but now divorce can result merely from a sense of dissatisfaction (as in no-fault divorce) and a sense of hope that one can find a more attractive alternative relationship. As a result of these differing (and higher) expectations and the greater likelihood of disappointment and frustration, individuals may have less commitment overall to their marriages and might be more inclined to initiate a divorce than was the case in earlier cohorts of married individuals.

The question then arises why marriage has remained so popular, despite the greater challenges to its vitality and longevity. Cherlin (2004) has suggested that the major advantage to marriage is what he labeled *enforceable trust*—that is, that marriage requires a public (i.e., legal) long-term commitment made in front of one's support network, whereas cohabitation requires only a private commitment that is relatively easier to break. The public nature of the process makes it at least somewhat more likely that partners will honor the commitments that they made to each other. We agree with Cherlin's view and add that another reason that marriage remains such a popular institution is that individuals have a somewhat naive view of marriage. They may believe that love conquers all and that passionate love will remain at the same high level throughout the marriage. They may not have a very realistic and clear sense of what marriage entails and how difficult it is to forge a strong bond, which might lead some individuals to enter into marriage prematurely before they understand the challenges that lie ahead as they forge a life together.

Societal views of divorce. Spouses' willingness to initiate and pursue a divorce is also related to societal views of divorce. The negative stigma associated with divorce has clearly lessened over time (Cherlin, 2004; Thornton & Young-DeMarco, 2001), although its downward course has leveled out in the past decade, and there remains considerable variability in social views of the acceptability of divorce. As Cherlin (2004) has observed, almost 50% of Americans believe that divorce should be more difficult to obtain, whereas only about 25% report believing that divorce should become easier to obtain; this difference has remained steady since around 1980. Further, there have been movements in many states, sometimes successful, to make divorce harder to obtain by increasing waiting periods or requiring counseling (Hawkins, Nock, Wilson, Sanchez, & Wright, 2002). Several states, including Louisiana, Arkansas, and Arizona (Hawkins et al., 2002), have also passed laws that allow people to choose a different type of marriage—called *covenant marriage.* Couples that choose a covenant marriage have a more difficult time obtaining a divorce, as they, in some states, have to wait longer to become divorced or need to receive counseling before the divorce can be granted. Very few couples are choosing this option (Hawkins et al., 2002), and no state has adopted a covenant marriage law since Arkansas did so.

Even though attitudes toward divorce do not seem to have become more positive in recent years, it is important to note that the current level of acceptance of divorce is at a very high level. For example, as presented in Cherlin (2004), about 80% of the young people in the Intergenerational Panel Study reported that they believe that divorce is acceptable even if the couple has children, and Inglehart (1997) reported that only 20% of American adults think that divorce is never justified. This relatively high level of acceptance of divorce presents a ceiling effect, which makes it challenging to reach higher acceptance levels in the future.

It is important to distinguish between acceptance and approval of divorce. Few, if any, individuals would claim that divorce is a desirable, preferred, or attractive option. As Cherlin (2004) has argued, the vast majority of adults, as well as adolescents, believe that staying married is the preferred alternative and that divorce is acceptable only as a last resort. In other words, although divorce is still viewed as undesirable and unfortunate, the long-term trend has been a greater acceptance of divorce as a way to end an unhealthy or unsatisfying marriage. However, despite this long-term trend, there have been a number of short-term periods, such as the current one, when there have been movements in some segments of society to view divorce as causally responsible for some of society's social ills and, therefore, to make divorce more difficult to obtain (see Hawkins et al., 2002; Popenoe, 1996; Thornton & Young-DeMarco, 2001).

Views of cohabitation. In addition to these changing views of marriage and divorce, values regarding cohabitation have become more accepting (Teachman, Tedrow, & Hall, 2006; Thornton & Young-DeMarco, 2001). Cohabitation had a clearly negative connotation in years past, as reflected by the terms that were (and in some circles, still are) used to describe it (e.g., shacking up, living in sin). However, cohabitation has clearly become increasingly accepted over time in two primary ways (Cherlin, 2004).

First, cohabitation is increasingly accepted as an alternative to marriage. Despite the steady interest in and devotion to the institution of marriage, an increasing proportion of individuals cohabit as an alternative to marriage. For many of these individuals, cohabitation is not perceived as an interim arrangement before eventually getting married; rather, the cohabiting arrangement is considered to be an end in itself. These individuals judge the quality and stability of their relationship based on such factors as the partners' level of commitment, love, and devotion to each other, rather than on the presence of a marriage license.

The second way that beliefs and practices related to cohabitation have changed is in the context following divorce. Divorced individuals are more likely to cohabit in their subsequent relationships than are individuals who have never been married, and they are more likely to cohabit following divorce than they were before their first marriage (Ganong, Coleman, & Hans, 2006). Individuals whose previous relationship ended in divorce or dissolution tend to hold more pragmatic and practical views of romantic relationships than do those who are in their first committed romantic relationship (Ganong et al., 2006). Because of the stressors associated with the experience of divorce (Fine & Harvey, 2006b; Harvey & Fine, 2004), divorced individuals may also be more cautious regarding getting married again. This greater pragmatism and cautiousness may lead them to reject the notion of legally getting married and, instead, to function together as a committed couple without a marriage certificate.

Critics of the greater acceptance of cohabitation cite research showing that cohabitation is associated with some negative child, adult, and relationship outcomes, such as a higher likelihood of divorce should the couple eventually marry (Cohan & Kleinbaum, 2002; Teachman et al., 2006). However, this well-publicized trend is reversing itself, as the greater risk of later divorce seems to be present primarily for those who have been serial cohabitors; Teachman (2003) found that premarital cohabitation was not associated with a higher risk of divorce if it was restricted to one's future spouse.

⧔ HISTORICAL CHANGES IN DIVORCE

The history surrounding divorce helps to place current divorce-related trends and experiences in context. Amato and Irving (2006) examined historical changes in divorce in three eras: the Colonial era (1620 to the Revolutionary War), the period between the Revolutionary War and the end of the 19th century, and the 20th century. Their analysis is instructive in identifying changes over time and in showing that there have been commonalities in some divorce-related trends over time.

Over the past 400 years, Amato and Irving (2006) identified the following general trends. First, although the rate of divorce in the United States has ebbed and flowed over time, the predominant pattern—beginning in the 17th century and continuing through the 20th century—has been a gradual increase in the divorce rate. The origins of current divorce rates—considered high by many—lie in social, legal, and interpersonal phenomena that are over 300 years old. Thus, because it represents a continuation, although an accelerated one, of earlier patterns, the well-documented increase in the divorce rate from the early 1960s until the early 1980s cannot solely be accounted for by recent social forces, such as the shift from fault-based to no-fault divorce. Theories and explanations of increases in the divorce rate have to take into account social forces dating back to the beginning of American society.

Second, the circumstances that the legal system and the general public regard as reasonable justifications for granting a divorce have expanded throughout American history. During the Colonial era, divorces were granted only for a limited number of what were considered rather extreme (and rare) circumstances, such as desertion and adultery. However, just as there are now meaningful differences among states in the grounds for divorce, as well as in other matters related to the legal aspects of divorce, Phillips (1991) has shown that there were also notable differences among the American colonies in these divorce-related areas.

Across colonies and later states, these grounds were defined substantially more broadly during the 19th and 20th centuries. For example, the meaning of cruelty, which previously referred to relatively severe forms of physical abuse in the early 1800s, was expanded later to include acts of emotional cruelty and unkindness.

An especially pronounced expansion of the grounds for divorce took place in the 1970s and early 1980s, when all states passed versions of no-fault divorce laws. No-fault divorce eliminated the need for one spouse to prove that the marriage contract had been violated, thereby removing (or at least reducing) the need for couples to make up or to exaggerate stories of infidelity and cruelty to satisfy the conditions of the law. Such laws made it possible for couples to divorce for virtually any reason under the rubric of irreconcilable differences. Moreover, unilateral no-fault divorce (available in most states) meant that one spouse could obtain a divorce without the approval or consent of the other spouse. This trend toward an expansion of justifiable conditions for divorce reflects both an ever increasing demand (particularly among those who are seeking a divorce) for making divorce legally easier to obtain (e.g., shorter or no waiting periods following filing, less expensive filing fees) and the rising expectations of what should characterize a good marriage. Over time, the trend has been to consider that a good marriage should meet not only the couple's financial, childbearing, and childrearing needs, but also the socioemotional and psychological needs of each spouse (see Cherlin, 2004).

Third, Amato and Irving (2006) documented the trend for wives to file for divorce more often than husbands. This gender difference existed throughout the Colonial era, the 19th century, and the 20th century, and it has continued into the 21st century. Possible explanations for this gender difference include that men are more likely than women to engage in serious forms of violence, both inside and outside of marriage (Felson, 2002); that men are more likely than women to abuse alcohol and other substances; that men are more likely than women to engage in infidelity (Hall & Fincham, 2006); and that, in the Colonial era through the 19th century, husbands were considerably more likely than wives to desert their families, largely because men had more opportunities for economic independence. Thus, for hundreds of years it has been more common for women than men to initiate divorce because of their spouses' cruelty, adultery, or substance abuse (Amato & Previti, 2003).

Readers should keep in mind, however, that the reasons why women are more likely to file for divorce are far more complex than the simple explanation that women are initiating divorce solely because their husbands have behaved badly. A family systems perspective alerts researchers to the likelihood that both parties have played a role in the deteriorating marital processes that eventually lead to one spouse— typically the wife—filing for divorce.

Another dimension of the complexity in identifying which spouse initiates the divorce is based on the notion that the actual filing for divorce is not equivalent to initiating the relationship dissolution process; the relative contributions of both spouses to the eventual dissolution of their relationship are complex, subtle, not easily identified, and begin long before the actual filing in court occurs. Previewing material in later chapters, the filing of the divorce papers reflects the culmination of a long series of events and needs to be considered as a part of the process of legally terminating the marriage as opposed to the key event signifying the legal end of the relationship. As an example, it is quite possible that one spouse may desire, at some level of consciousness, to end the marriage, but does not actually wish to be the one identified as filing for divorce. Thus, that spouse may engage in behaviors such as emotional abuse, infidelity (either emotional or sexual or both), or withdrawal that may eventually push the other spouse to the point where he or she feels that filing for divorce is the best (and perhaps only) available option.

As discussed further in Chapters 5 and 6, Hopper (2001) and Rollie and Duck (2006) have suggested that the actual legal filing of the divorce papers is only one among a long series of divorce-related events. In addition, these researchers suggest that each partner constructs a narrative of the dissolution of the marriage and that this story serves to meet both personal and social needs. Because of the constructed nature of these narratives of the divorce process, Hopper's work suggests that it is extremely difficult, if not impossible, to accurately depict what actually happened leading up to the divorce.

Fourth, Amato and Irving (2006) concluded that divorce has always been controversial in American society. For example, during the Colonial era, there were clear differences between New England and the southern colonies regarding whether divorce should be allowed at all. After World War I, many individuals (including many social scientists) claimed that the family was in danger, with harmful consequences for children and society in general. During the 1980s and 1990s, this debate emerged yet again among policy makers, the media, the general public, and family scholars (Popenoe, 1993; Stacey, 1993; Whitehead, 1993). Currently, not only are there widely publicized debates regarding such crucial matters as the effects that divorce has on children, but also there are legal debates regarding the extent to which public policy should make marriage a stronger institution or render divorce more difficult to obtain. It is interesting to note that Amato and Irving found that many of the arguments that are made both in favor of and against divorce today are quite similar, if not identical, in rhetoric and substance, to arguments made in previous eras.

In addition to the historical trends identified by Amato and Irving, we offer some additional historical patterns. A fifth historical trend is that public policy toward divorce (and marriage) is intimately intertwined with religious values and institutions. As one illustration, Fine and Fine (1994) reviewed trends in divorce laws in five Western countries and found that countries that are heavily influenced by the Catholic Church (e.g., Spain) have been more hesitant to allow divorce to occur at all, and once it was allowed, it has been made relatively difficult to obtain. Divorce is even more strongly stigmatized in countries with Muslim governance (Al-Krenawi & Graham, 1998; Cohen & Savaya, 2003).

Sixth, there has been and continues to be considerable variation in divorce rates, laws, beliefs, and attitudes within the United States, and presumably within other countries as well. Reflective of the value placed on states' rights in the United States, family law, in general, and divorce law, in particular, are determined at the state level with very little uniformity dictated by federal mandates. Thus, each state determines its own laws pertaining to divorce, and the fact that there is variability in these laws from state to state (Mahoney, 2006) suggests that there are considerably different beliefs about divorce, how easy it should be to obtain a divorce, where children should live following divorce (i.e., custody), patterns of contact between parents and children (i.e., visitation or parenting time), child support payments, and how property should be divided.

For example, Pirog (Pirog & Ziol-Guest, 2006; Pirog-Good, 1993) has shown that formulas determining child support awards differ substantially from state to state, and that these differences are not due solely to state and regional variations in the cost of living. Thus, children's (and their residential parents') financial well-being depends to some extent on the state in which they reside. Even the way that child support awards are determined varies from state to state (Pirog & Ziol-Guest, 2006), virtually guaranteeing that the size of these awards will differ across the country. As another example, there is considerable variation in divorce rates in different regions of the United States. Despite being more conservative ideologically, states in the western part of the United States, with the possible exceptions of California, Washington, and Oregon, have higher divorce rates than do more liberal states in the eastern United States (Centers for Disease Control, 2005; Rodrigues, Hall, & Fincham, 2006), perhaps reflecting the supposedly more independent and pioneering spirit of individuals who migrated westward during U.S. history. Also, despite being more liberal in the aggregate, regional variation is again reflected in the finding that northern states have slightly lower divorce rates than do southern states.

A final noteworthy trend is that there has been a small, but steady, decline in the divorce rate since the early 1980s (Kreider, 2007). From a peak of 5.3 per 1,000 individuals in 1981, the rate declined throughout the 1980s and has remained steady at about 4.7.

Some scholars have suggested that the recent decline indicates that the divorce rate hit its ceiling in the early 1980s and that it is unlikely to return upward to new highs. Perhaps the wealth of relationship advice (e.g., from Dr. Phil, self-help books) that is currently available and easily accessible to individuals in romantic relationships has had some success in reducing the probability of marital dissolution.

〉〉〉 CROSS-CULTURAL CONTEXT

As we noted in Chapter 1, approximately 40% of marriages will ultimately end in divorce (Hurley, 2005). Amato and Irving (2006) estimated that currently about 2% of marriages end in divorce each year and suggested that this rate has decreased slightly since the early 1980s.

However, this overall rate masks considerable variability in divorce rates across a variety of cultural and demographic subgroups (Bramlett & Mosher, 2001). Here, we will provide a brief illustrative review of variations along two of these dimensions—race-ethnicity and age.

Race-ethnicity. Although a smaller proportion of African Americans marry than European Americans, a much higher percentage of African American marriages end in divorce than is the case for European Americans (Orbuch & Brown, 2006). In the 1990s, approximately 47% of African American marriages resulted in separation within 10 to 15 years, compared with 28% of European American marriages (Cherlin, 1998; Tucker & Mitchell-Kernan, 1995). The divorce rate for Latinos is lower than that for both

European Americans and African Americans (Umaña-Taylor & Alfaro, 2006), although there are important differences among Latino subgroups. For example, divorce rates are approximately twice as high for Puerto-Rican-origin couples as for Mexican-origin couples (Umaña-Taylor & Alfaro, 2006). Further, rates of divorce for Asian Americans are the lowest of any racial-ethnic group (Teachman et al., 2006).

However, a finding pertaining to Latino married couples, but not one that is unique to Latino couples, illustrates the important point made earlier that not all dissolved relationships culminate in divorce. Despite their lower divorce rates, Latinos appear to have higher rates of using separation as a way of dissolving marital relationships than do other racial-ethnic groups (Umaña-Taylor & Alfaro, 2006). Divorce is only one way, albeit a legal way, to terminate one's relationship; the spouses also may separate from one another indefinitely and remain married.

Age. Divorce rates are considerably higher for younger married individuals than for older married persons. For women, in the aggregate, the divorce rate has a consistent, linear, inverse slope as the woman's age increases. For example, in 1995, divorce rates were highest for women ages 15 to 19 years (48.6 per 1,000 married women), and they were lowest for married women over age 65 (1.4 per 1,000). For men, the age-related pattern is very similar with one exception. Men ages 20 to 24 years had the highest divorce rate (50.2 per 1,000) in 1995, and then the rate dropped precipitously as it did for women until it reached 2.1 for married men over the age of 65 years. Men in the 15 to 19 age range had a 32.8 per 1,000 divorce rate. As a result, most divorcing men (almost 67%) and divorcing women (almost 75%) were under age 40 at the time of their divorce, with the modal age-group being 30 to 34 years of age for men and 25 to 29 years of age for women (Clarke, 1995). In some sense, then, divorce is a process that affects more young people than older persons, although the age at divorce has increased by more than 3 years since 1975.

\\ LEGAL CONTEXT

Because the divorce process includes a legal component, the legal context is a critical one to consider. In this section, we address several legal issues related to divorce, including grounds for divorce and a number of matters concerning the aftermath of the divorce, including spousal maintenance or alimony, division of marital assets, child support, child visitation, and child custody. All of these legal issues are governed by state rather than federal law, and there is considerable variability from state to state in laws regulating divorce. As described in the following sections, laws governing divorce and its aftermath have undergone major changes in every state since the 1970s. According to Mahoney (2006) and Mason, Fine, and Carnochan (2001), in aggregate, these changes can be referred to as the no-fault divorce revolution or divorce revolution, with a counterrevolution gaining increased support. Because in-depth treatments of divorce laws and variations from state to state are provided on a regular basis elsewhere (the *Family Law Quarterly* provides state-by-state annual updates on a variety of issues pertaining to family law, including all aspects of divorce), our coverage focuses on general U.S. trends rather than an exhaustive presentation of all legal variations across the states.

Grounds for divorce. Before the 1970s, the laws in most states granted a divorce only when marital fault on the part of one spouse could be documented. The most common fault grounds included adultery, cruelty, desertion, and imprisonment for a crime (Gregory, Swisher, & Wolf, 2001, sec. 8.03[B]). In this system of fault, the spouse filing for divorce had to claim and prove to the satisfaction of the judge or divorce court that the other spouse had performed one or more of the behaviors. If the accused spouse disputed the claim that he or she had engaged in these behaviors and was able to prove his or her innocence, the judge would deny the divorce. If the judge concluded that the filing spouse's allegations were correct, even though the other spouse denied them, the judge would grant the divorce over the objection of the nonfiling spouse.

In cases in which both parties wanted to terminate their relationship, a dilemma sometimes arose under fault-based systems. If neither partner had engaged in behavior qualifying as a ground for divorce, the only way that such a couple could obtain a divorce was to misrepresent what happened in their marriage so that it qualified as a ground for divorce (Krause & Meyer, 2003). With the increased number of divorces occurring in the 1960s, this major criticism—that spouses felt forced to fabricate misbehavior that met the criteria for divorce in fault-based laws—became much stronger. Many felt that laws that in any way encouraged lying were unacceptable.

This criticism of fault-based laws led to the no-fault divorce revolution in the 1970s and early 1980s. Across the country, state legislatures made major changes in the laws governing the grounds for divorce. The new laws introduced what were termed no-fault grounds, such as that the marriage had reached a state of irretrievable breakdown or that there were irreconcilable differences between the spouses (Mason et al., 2001). Despite the fact that eventually all states adopted some version of no-fault divorce (see Vlosky & Monroe, 2002), there were nevertheless substantial variations from state to state (Mahoney, 2006; Mason et al., 2001). Some states replaced fault-based laws with no-fault laws, while other states merely added no-fault options to the already existing fault-based laws. In addition, some states adopted waiting periods with differing lengths of separation before the divorce could be granted, while other states had no such waiting periods.

What happens if one spouse does not agree to the divorce? Even in no-fault divorces, such cases become considerably more complex if one partner contests the grounds for divorce. However, as Mahoney (2006) suggests, even though the spouse contesting the divorce can attempt to provide evidence that the marriage is still vital, the contesting spouse can delay, but not prevent, the divorce, unless the other partner changes his or her mind regarding the divorce.

What is the current legal context regarding the grounds for divorce? As we briefly described earlier, societal views and laws have historically ebbed and flowed along a continuum defined on one pole by the notions that divorce is a private matter between two individuals and that it should be relatively easy to obtain and, on the other pole, by the views that marriage and family life are of central importance to any society, that the government has an interest in reducing the prevalence of divorce, and that, therefore, divorce should be relatively difficult to obtain. In recent years, social views and laws have moved toward the divorce should be made more difficult to obtain end of the continuum. Many have claimed that no-fault divorce laws have established a system of divorce-on-demand, which allows couples to divorce quickly without working to sustain their marriage (Emery, 1999; Mahoney, 2006; Mason et al., 2001). Furthermore, critics have suggested that many social ills, especially those relating to poverty in single-parent families, are exacerbated by how easy it is to obtain a divorce (Popenoe, 1996).

Reflective of the change toward more conservative views of marriage and divorce, many states have proposed a return to fault-based divorce (Mahoney, 2006). As noted earlier in this chapter, in three states, the state legislature has established covenant marriage as an option for couples who marry. Among the differences between covenant marriages and other marriages in Louisiana is that a covenant marriage requires a more fault-based set of grounds for divorce (La. Rev. Stat. Ann. § 9:972).

In addition, some states have proposed extending the waiting period between the time of filing for divorce and when the divorce can be granted. The legislative proposals to make divorce more difficult to obtain have been controversial and, hence, have had only limited success in state legislatures. As discussed earlier, the divorce counterrevolution has made relatively few gains.

Spousal maintenance. Spousal maintenance, or alimony, involves one partner—typically the man—paying the other—typically the woman—a specified sum of money for either a set amount of time or indefinitely into the future. Under fault-based laws, alimony was paid by men as a continuation of their obligation to support their spouse during the marriage. The amount of alimony awarded was greater to the extent that the husband engaged in behaviors qualifying as marital fault and to the extent that the man had greater earning potential and resources than did the woman.

In the past 30 years, the legal theory underlying alimony, now termed *spousal maintenance*, has changed. Instead of spousal maintenance being based in punishment for undesirable behavior or for past inequities in socioeconomic status, the primary goal of spousal maintenance became ending, in a fair and just manner, the economic dependence that one spouse developed on the other during the marriage. This theory of rehabilitative alimony found widespread acceptance early in the no-fault era (Krause & Meyer, 2003, pp. 262–263). According to this theory, when appropriate, the best interests of at least the maintenance-receiving ex-spouse (and maybe even the maintenance-paying ex-spouse) would be supported by awarding maintenance for a limited time period to allow the recipient to improve his or her future income potential. Proponents of this theory considered the increasing financial opportunities for women in the workplace as support for their argument that women should receive maintenance only until they could reestablish their economic independence. (For an excellent review of the issues involved in alimony, see Shehan, Berardo, Owens, & Berardo, 2002.)

A related aspect of divorce law pertains to property distribution. Equitable distribution of property laws were introduced in most states during the no-fault revolution, which gave divorce courts the authority to redistribute spouses' assets. The underlying legal theory was that the availability of a property redistribution option would often eliminate the need for long-term maintenance. Needless to say, property redistribution cannot occur in instances when the couple has few assets to divide.

Further, property redistribution is not helpful for spouses who need the liquidity provided by monthly (or lump-sum) payments.

Most recently, there has been an even greater move away from the concept of alimony. In the *Principles of the Law of Family Dissolution*, the American Law Institute (ALI) rejected the concept of alimony itself (Mahoney, 2006). The *Principles* proposed a substitute for alimony called *compensatory payments*, which is solely designed to compensate spouses for certain types of financial losses resulting from divorce (ALI, 2002, chap. 5). A former spouse's eligibility for compensatory payments from the other would be determined by a series of supposedly objective criteria, such as, for example, a large difference in the spouses' incomes following divorce after a marriage of some specified length. The size and duration of compensatory payments would be determined by clear guidelines, similar to those determining child support awards. As is the case with child support, the judge would have the authority to modify the compensatory payment amount if he or she judged that an adjustment was necessary to achieve fairness to both parties. To date, although no state legislature has changed its alimony or spousal maintenance statute by adopting the compensatory payment doctrine (Mahoney, 2006), the ALI proposal has reopened and reinvigorated the discussion about how to achieve financial equity between former spouses.

Child support. The state laws governing child support underwent considerable change during the 1980s, when Congress felt the need to become involved in child support. Before this time, child support laws provided the family court judge with considerable discretion to determine the appropriate amount of financial support that each parent should provide to the child. The federal government became involved because of widespread dissatisfaction with the lack of consistency in child support awards across cases, the small size of many child support awards that were established by state court judges, and the high rate of noncompliance by parents—mostly fathers—in paying their child support (Pirog & Ziol-Guest, 2006).

Even though the federal government has no authority to pass child support laws or to require states to pass particular laws, in the 1980s, Congress exerted pressure on the states to modify their child support laws and policies by passing laws that would cause a state to lose billions of dollars in federal support if it did not make designated changes in its child support legislation. Not surprisingly, with the financial stakes so high, all states made the designated changes in their child support laws (Morgan, 1996 & Suppl. 2001, sec. 1.02[a][b]).

The changes "encouraged" by the federal government fall into two major categories. First, each state developed numerical guidelines to establish the amount of child support awards. The theory was that some of the inappropriate variability in child support award amounts (e.g., two families in similar situations having vastly different child support awards) would be eliminated if courts were forced to follow clear numerical formulas, unless there were clear extenuating reasons to deviate from the formula (Morgan, 1996 & Suppl. 2001, sec. 1.02[e]). In addition to the determination of the child support award amount, the guidelines also had to determine how to divide the obligation between the child's parents.

The second change indirectly mandated by federal intervention during the 1980s and 1990s involved the enforcement of child support orders. In response to evidence that many court-ordered child support awards were not paid, the federal government indirectly mandated that states establish a variety of mechanisms to improve collection rates (Krause & Meyer, 2003). Now, every state provides a number of mechanisms to collect child support awards, including establishing easier ways to garnish the obligated parent's wages-income, requiring the support-paying parent to have his or her child support awards automatically deducted from his or her paycheck, and judicial authority to require the obligated parent to post a bond or other security to guarantee regular support payments (Mahoney, 2006).

An area in which the federal government deliberately did not take a position involved divorced parents' responsibility for the costs of their children's higher education. In first-marriage families, state laws clearly state that parents are not legally obligated to support their child during the years of higher education following the child's 18th birthday. However, with the rationale being that divorced parents—primarily nonresidential parents—are presumed to be less likely to pay for the costs of their child's higher education than are married parents, many states have empowered divorce courts to order divorced parents to support a child beyond the age of majority while the child pursues a higher education (Morgan, 1996 & Suppl. 2001, sec. 4.05[d]). Because Congress left this issue to the discretion of the states, there is still considerable variation in state laws regarding divorced parents' responsibilities to pay for their children's higher education. Many states impose no such obligation, while others do only under certain circumstances (e.g., the obligation lasts only until the child is 21 or 22 years old; the child must be a full-time student).

Child custody. All states have laws regarding the custody of minor children following the divorce of their parents. Determinations must be made about two primary topics involving the postdivorce custody of children—where children will physically reside (i.e., physical custody) and which parent(s) will make the important decisions affecting the children's future (i.e., legal custody). Laws in this area have been substantially modified in the last several decades (see Mason, 2000).

State custody laws provide standards to guide judges in making decisions about the future parenting of children following divorce. Not only are these standards used by judges to make custody decisions, but they are also used in the majority of cases that are determined through mediation and negotiation between the parents and not decided by a judge. Mnookin and Kornhauser (1979) referred to this as "negotiating in the shadow of the law," suggesting that the law provides the background that helps structure discussions between the parents regarding how to best care for their children following divorce.

Before the 1970s, the gender of the divorcing parents played a major role in determining which parent would have custody of the children following divorce (Mahoney, 2006). Based on the theory (the tender years doctrine) that minor children, especially young ones, needed their mothers on a daily basis to a greater degree than they needed their fathers, the mother was generally awarded custody of minor children. These gender-based laws also were based on the assumption that one (typically the mother) and not both parents should be the primary custodial parent.

In the 1970s, sole custody typically entailed both physical and legal custody. The noncustodial parent (usually the father) typically had a specified amount of time to spend with the child, known as *visitation*, had some limited decision-making authority, and was required to make child support payments. This model of child custody was the "default," unless special circumstances suggested that some alternative solution was preferable.

The gender-based tender years doctrine was widely criticized during the 1970s, and custody laws were substantially changed as a result. In particular, gender was rejected as a basis for determining postdivorce living and financial arrangements. In its place, the "best interests of the child" standard was adopted. This standard mandates that courts and judges consider, on a case-by-case basis, all relevant circumstances regarding both parents and children in making decisions that are in the children's best interests. Thus, the children's needs, rather than the parents' gender, were to be the most important consideration in determining custody, visitation, and support orders. Because orders were to be determined on a case-by-case basis and because the number of relevant circumstances that need to be considered is almost infinite, the primary difficulty associated with this standard was that there was a lack of certainty and predictability in legal decisions, especially when both parents were "fit" and loving. As a result, both family court judges and parents felt that court orders were at least somewhat arbitrary. Since then, and with the aim of inserting more certainty into the process, laws have changed so that divorce-related court orders are more structured and predictable.

Below, we review four of these recent developments in child custody law. First, laws have changed so that the most commonly used custody guideline, which was recently drafted in the *Principles of the Law of Family Dissolution*, proposes that each parent's postdivorce parenting responsibilities would be determined on the basis of each parent's predivorce involvement with the children (ALI, 2002, sec. 2.08). This standard gives weight to the parents' past parenting behaviors in determining the family environment that would be in the children's best interests following the divorce. The theory underlying this standard assumes that continuity in parenting arrangements from before until after marital disruption best facilitates children's adjustment to this stressor.

Second, joint custody has been introduced as a custody presumption in many states. Joint custody is based on the notion that children will adjust most effectively to divorce to the extent that both parents are actively involved in their lives. Joint custody allows both parents to retain some decision-making authority over the child's well-being, unlike the more traditional custodial-noncustodial parental model that preceded it. In addition, not only may legal custody be shared, but there is also the legal option for children's physical custody to be shared between the two parents' new homes. In such instances, the child literally has two homes and divides his or her living time between them. States vary in terms of how strongly joint custody is encouraged, ranging from presuming joint custody unless circumstances dictate otherwise to providing joint custody as one among many custodial options (Mahoney, 2006).

The changes in custody guidelines have led to some welcome changes in the language used to describe children's living arrangements following divorce. Instead of *custody* and *visitation*, terms such as *parenting, parenting plans, parenting time, children's residence(s)*, and *parental decision making* have gained favor, to some extent, in many parts of the country. These new terms are welcomed because *custody* suggests that children are the property of their parents and *visitation* suggests that nonresidential parents are guests in their children's lives who drop in and spend time with them on occasion. Nevertheless, the more traditional terms are still often used by parents, lawyers, judges, and scholars alike, because they are familiar and widely understood.

Third, modern custody law has imposed certain restrictions on factors that the courts are able to consider. Although the best interests of the child standard encourages judges to consider all relevant factors related to the children, parents (and their lawyers) have successfully made the argument in many cases that certain variables, such as the parent's sexual orientation, religion, or race, should not be considered in custody cases. The rationale for not considering such issues may be based on the state or federal constitution, state-level policy, or the belief that a particular factor is not relevant to the welfare of children. With the exception of race (*Palmore v. Sidoti*, 1984), very few rules regarding factors that must be excluded from consideration have been passed (Krause & Meyer, 2003). In particular cases, state legislatures and courts have been reluctant to limit the range of factors that may be considered in determining the best interests of the child. Thus, for example, in most states, a parent's sexual orientation or religious-spiritual practices may be considered by the judge, if there is sufficient evidence that the child's well-being has been affected by these factors, or any other factors that are shown to be relevant.

Finally, many states have required divorcing parents to become more proactive in planning for their children's best interests and to become better educated regarding how to help their children cope with divorce. The more systematic and proactive planning process is reflected in the requirement that divorcing parents develop a parenting plan early in the process of obtaining a divorce. The parenting plan is designed to reflect the parents' agreement on issues pertaining to raising their children, including both long-term issues such as who will pay for college expenses and short-term issues such as when each parent will be able to spend time with the children (Fine et al., 1999). States differ in how the process of developing a parenting plan is carried out, but the end result in almost all states is a written document that details how the parents will care for their children.

The educational requirement is reflected in parenting education classes for divorcing parents that are required in many counties in most states in the country (Blaisure & Geasler, 2006). Such programs are typically for parents rather than for children, consist of a single several hour long session, attempt to increase parents' awareness of their children's reactions to divorce, emphasize the importance of keeping children out of the middle of their parents' disputes, and teach parents skills to help their children cope with divorce more effectively. Although these programs have considerable promise, their widespread adoption and use has far outstripped their empirical support—there are relatively few studies that have demonstrated their efficacy. Educating parents regarding how to help their children cope more effectively with divorce is such an intuitively appealing idea, however, that most jurisdictions in the United States have been willing to mandate that parents attend educational sessions. These parenting education classes, and particularly the curriculum and videotapes that underlie them, have become part of the divorce industry (Harvey & Fine, 2004).

Collaborative divorce. In response to well-publicized limitations of the adversarial legal process, a number of alternative legal approaches have been developed to address disputes in a less adversarial way, including mediation and, most recently, collaborative divorce. In essence, collaborative divorce is based on the notion that better and longer lasting resolutions will be achieved if the parties collaborate to seek mutually acceptable solutions rather than fight with one another to maximize one's own personal gain (see www.collaborativedivorce.net). In collaborative divorce, all parties agree not to pursue litigation while the negotiations unfold. To ensure that the lawyers engaged in collaborative divorce have no incentive to fail, the parties and their lawyers agree that the lawyers will withdraw from the case if the collaborative divorce process is unsuccessful and if litigation ensues. Although similar in its goals, collaborative divorce differs from mediation in that, in collaborative divorce, each party retains his or her own personal counsel, while in mediation, an objective third party, the mediator, helps the parties reach a compromised solution.

Because of its relative recency (the idea originated by a Minnesota lawyer, Stu Webb, in 1990), there are few empirical studies about the efficacy of collaborative divorce. However, lawyers and clients, on an anecdotal level, consistently report that it can be quicker, less expensive, and less distressing than the typical adversarial process. Intuitively, this approach is very appealing for many clients, but perhaps the key caveat is that it is not appropriate for all couples: Many spouses or couples are not good candidates for collaborative divorce because they do not have the necessary collaborative conflict resolution skills, the necessary personal characteristics, or the necessary relational dynamics to engage in an effective cooperative process. For such couples, the typical adversarial process may be the only viable option.

Legal aspects of divorce in other Western and non-Western countries. In their review of divorce laws and changes in divorce laws in five Western countries (the United States, France, England, Wales, and Germany), Fine and Fine (1994) observed that, although there were important differences in how some countries have changed their divorce laws, there were a number of common trends that have occurred across the five Western countries they examined. These trends are helpful to review because they show that many patterns observed in the United States have also occurred in a broader cross-national context. First, divorce has become increasingly easy to obtain. Second, spousal support-maintenance has been awarded less frequently. Third, a range of efforts have been made to increase the amount of child support awards and to improve compliance rates. Fourth, laws have increasingly accepted and encouraged shared parental decision-making authority (e.g., joint custody).

In Western societies, these trends have tended to continue into the present (Cretney, 2003). In addition, although divorce laws and practices were quite different in some Asian countries, there is evidence that the same patterns and trends noted above in Western countries are increasingly characterizing these countries as well (Faison, 1994; Huang, 2007). For example, after historically having very low divorce rates, the current divorce rate in China has risen to an estimated 50%. Before attempting to understand the effects that divorce has on particular individuals, even though divorce laws are becoming more similar across countries over time, it is essential to take into consideration the legal context surrounding those individuals, including the culture and country in which they reside.

⚞ CONCLUSIONS

In this chapter, we have provided an overview of various contexts that affect the experience of and reactions to divorce. In particular, we have reviewed the attitudinal, historical, cross-cultural, and legal contexts affecting the divorce process—all contexts that are visually portrayed in Figure 2.1 in Chapter 2. Our review has demonstrated that some aspects of divorce have a long history (e.g., women filing for divorce more commonly than men; the stigma associated with divorce), whereas other developments are more recent (e.g., the relatively high divorce rate of 40%; an increasing acceptance of cohabitation). As we now proceed to consider a number of substantive issues pertaining to divorce in subsequent chapters, it is important to keep in mind that many "contemporary" aspects of divorce are not unique to this era or generation, but reflect ongoing trends that have ebbed and flowed for many years. Most important, perhaps, is the lesson that the context affecting divorce is ever-changing. Any depiction of this context, such as that provided in this chapter, is merely a snapshot portrayal of a moving target.

In the chapters that follow, we consider variation in predivorce, divorce, and postdivorce processes and outcomes for children and adults. It is important to be sensitive to the various contexts depicted in this chapter and to realize the fluid contextual environment in which divorce plays out. For example, children's adjustment to divorce is intimately affected by current trends in child custody laws. Further, as these laws change (e.g., more strongly encouraging joint custody and, thus, active involvement by both parents), it is likely that children's reactions and adjustment to divorce will likewise change.

It is also important to acknowledge that the contexts affecting divorce are not uniform for all children and adults. Some contexts affect some individuals differently than others, depending on a wide array of factors, such as race, socioeconomic status, gender, sexual orientation, the state in which one lives, and age. Thus, the wide variation in experiences and reactions that we emphasize in subsequent chapters is partly due to the heterogeneity in divorce-related contexts.

PART II

The Divorce Process and Its Multiple Pathways

5

Variation in Predivorce Family Environments and Trajectories

It's such a gradual thing. I don't think I ever wanted to admit that I wasn't in love with him. . . . But romantically I didn't want him to touch me, and we fought continuously. And I preferred not to be around him unless we were with a group of people, and then we couldn't fight. I think all of a sudden one day I realized, "I'm just not in love with this man."

At that time I was thinking that I didn't know if I loved her. I had lived with this so long. I didn't know what real love was. . . . If she left me, I wouldn't die. (Kayser & Rao, 2006, p. 210)

Most marriages endure prolonged periods of unhappiness, growing apart, poor communication, tension, and conflict prior to any discussions of divorce. Paradoxically, for many couples the start of the divorce process may coincide with the transition to marriage. The greatest risk of divorce occurs following the newlywed period (Rodrigues et al., 2006), with about half of all first marriages ending in divorce within the first 8 years of marriage (U.S. Census Bureau, 2007). A second peak occurs in midlife, roughly corresponding with the period when parents have young teenage children (Gottman & Levenson, 2000). What happens in the marital relationship that leads couples to divorce? How do their actions as partners, and often as parents, set in motion a process of marital breakdown? How are parent–child interactions affected during the period of marital decline?

In this chapter, we present information on how predivorce dynamics and interactions affect a variety of family relationships, including marital and parent–child relationships. Chapter 6 provides a more focused look at marital separation, the decision to separate, variations in separation and uncoupling processes, and accompanying changes in social networks. To accomplish our goals for this chapter, we begin by describing a range of factors that erode marital quality and thus increase the chances of divorce. Then we examine variation in marital and family dynamics in divorcing families. We summarize research on marital processes associated with marital breakdown, and we highlight the widely varying pathways and timetables leading to marital dissolution. Throughout the chapter, and consistent with our emphasis on the dynamic and fluid nature of the divorce process illustrated in Chapter 2 (Figure 2.1), we suggest that the process of marital decline is nonlinear—that is, there is an uncertainty to the process, it ebbs and flows, and its direction might best be described as circuitous. We also discuss uncertainties and ambiguities surrounding the "dark" side of divorce, including psychological and physical aggression. Research evidence indicates that psychological aggression and physical aggression are common in marriage and are associated with marital decline. Finally, we examine some common dynamics of parent–child relationships prior to divorce, including adults' and children's diminishing social and emotional adjustment in the period leading up to marital dissolution.

⚒ CAUSES AND CORRELATES OF DIVORCE

Usually, there is not just one reason for divorce; most marriages that end in divorce exhibit several risk factors. It is also important to keep in mind that although research designs that are typically used in divorce research (discussed in greater detail in Chapter 3) are valuable in identifying factors associated with an increased probability of divorce (i.e., correlates of divorce), it is much more difficult to isolate the *causes* of divorce. Viewed broadly, routinized daily activities (notably including competing demands related to employment, household labor, and caring for family members), along with both anticipated and unanticipated everyday hassles (e.g., an accident, a denial of a credit application, a sick parent, or an injured child) create chronic stressors for family life and marital relationships (Helms & Demo, 2005; Serido, Almeida, & Wethington, 2004). Combined with a cultural context in which there are very high expectations for marriage, many marital relationships are vulnerable to conflict, dissatisfaction, and divorce.

In a thoughtful review of the research literature on factors predicting divorce, Rodrigues et al. (2006) outline three types of influences: a) sociodemographic and life-course factors, b) individual difference factors, and c) relationship process factors. Sociodemographic and life-course variables can be viewed as distal factors that affect the likelihood that problems will develop in the marital relationship (Amato & Rogers, 1997). For example, high unemployment, poverty, low levels of education and family income, and other oppressive social conditions create stressors on marriage that, in turn, contribute to a higher divorce rate for African Americans than for White Americans (Orbuch, Veroff, Hassan, & Horrocks, 2002). Likewise, although there is substantial within-group variation among Latino populations (Umaña-Taylor & Alfaro, 2006), Latinos and African Americans are much more likely than Whites to separate without ever divorcing. Other sociodemographic and life-course factors associated with an increased risk of divorce include living in more densely populated or urban areas, living or working in areas where there are numerous relationship alternatives to the current partner, premarital cohabitation (especially serial cohabitation), premarital childbearing, early age at marriage, shorter marital duration, remarriage, low levels of religious participation, low levels of support for the relationship from family and friends, and experiencing parental divorce as a child (Amato & Rogers, 1997; Bryant & Conger, 1999; Rodrigues et al., 2006; South, Trent, & Shen, 2001).

Marriages are also more susceptible to divorce when spouses exhibit specific behaviors and individual characteristics—the second set of risk factors. Theory and research suggest that personality and mental health problems such as antisocial behavior, alcohol or drug use, neuroticism, negative affect, and psychiatric disorders detract from marital interaction and marital quality, and increase the likelihood of divorce (Amato & Previti, 2003; Karney & Bradbury, 1995; Leonard & Roberts, 1998; Rodrigues et al., 2006). In a study examining specific reasons that people reported for why their marriages ended in divorce, many of the most commonly cited reasons involved factors associated with personality: Incompatibility ranked as the second most frequent cause, and problems with alcohol or drug use ranked third, followed by growing apart and experiencing personality problems (Amato & Previti, 2003). (Infidelity was the most commonly mentioned perceived cause.)

A third set of factors that predict marital dissolution involve proximal marital relationship processes. As noted above, Amato and Previti (2003) found that the most common cause of divorce reported by formerly married individuals was infidelity, with 25% of women and 15% of men citing it as a main factor. Emotional or sexual involvement outside the relationship casts a cloud over the marriage and precipitates anger, self-doubt, and major depressive episodes among spouses of unfaithful individuals (Buunk, 1995; Cano & O'Leary, 2000; Hall & Fincham, 2006). An important question is whether infidelity is a cause of marital dissolution or whether it is a symptom of other problems in the marriage. For example, some other relationship problems that are commonly identified as causes of divorce include lack of communication, losing a sense of closeness, not feeling loved or appreciated, and physical or mental abuse (Amato & Previti, 2003; Gigy & Kelly, 1992). Any of these difficulties in the marital relationship, perhaps in combination with personality problems and chronic stressors such as those described earlier, may predispose individuals to infidelity, which in turn increases the risk of divorce (Amato & Rogers, 1997; Hall & Fincham, 2006).

Other types of hurtful and abusive interactions also serve to undermine intimacy in marriage. For example, there is evidence that criticism, betrayal, disassociation, and teasing provoke hurt feelings and relational distancing (Leary, Springer, Negel, Ansell, & Evans, 1998; Vangelisti, 2006). Gottman's (1993, 1994; Gottman, Coan, Carrere, & Swanson, 1998) influential research using detailed microanalytic coding of laboratory observations suggests that the frequency of positive affect in marital conflict interactions (e.g., interest, affection, humor, and excitement) and the presence and frequency of four specific negative interaction patterns—criticism, defensiveness, contempt, and stonewalling (the "4 Horsemen of the Apocalypse")—considered collectively, can predict divorce with an accuracy exceeding 90%. However, some scholars have cautioned that prediction studies, including those of Gottman and colleagues, are characterized by several methodological limitations that lead to overstated predictions (e.g., see Heyman & Smith Slep, 2001; Stanley, Bradbury, & Markman, 2000). Nonetheless, subsequent work found that the occurrence of the four negative behaviors (i.e., criticism, defensiveness, contempt, and stonewalling) strongly predicted early-occurring divorces (couples married a mean of 7 years before divorcing), whereas later divorces (couples married a mean of 14 years) were best predicted by the absence of positive affect (affection-caring, humor, interest-curiosity, and joy-enthusiasm) (Gottman & Levenson, 2000).

Other studies that followed newlywed couples over time corroborate the importance of positive, affectionate behaviors early in marriage and the destructive role of negative behaviors. Huston and colleagues found that marriages that ended in quick divorces (i.e., those occurring after 2 years of marriage) were characterized by lower levels of love, fewer affectionate acts, more ambivalence, and more negative behaviors (Huston, Caughlin, Houts, Smith, & George, 2001), and Kurdek (2002) found that decreases in love, liking, and trust over the first 4 years of marriage predicted separation by the 8th year of marriage. Another observational study using a prospective design and a sample of couples who were married a mean of 18 years demonstrated that unhappy marriages were characterized by spousal hostility (measured as angry, critical, defiant, rejecting, inconsiderate, and obnoxious behavior) and that these behaviors predicted both subsequent marital distress and divorce (Matthews, Wickrama, & Conger, 1996). In sum, a wide range of hurtful behaviors appear to erode spouses' feelings for one another beginning in the earliest years of marriage, activating a process of gradual marital decline for some couples, and precipitous decline for others.

The demand-withdraw communication pattern during marital conflict has also received considerable attention as a precursor of marital dissatisfaction and dissolution (Eldridge & Christensen, 2002; Gottman & Notarius, 2000). This pattern involves one partner making demands (e.g., emotional appeals, nagging, complaints) and the other partner withdrawing from the interaction (e.g., not responding, avoiding eye contact, becoming defensive, changing the subject, physically leaving the room). Hetherington (2003) used the term *pursuer-distancer* to describe these relationships, and she found that they had the highest risks of divorce among five common marital relationship types she identified. Although most commonly studied as a wife-demand–husband-withdraw dynamic, emerging evidence suggests that traditional gender stereotypes paint an incomplete and inaccurate picture of processes associated with marital distress and that greater attention needs to be devoted to the context in which either partner issues demands or withdraws.

More specifically, there is evidence that demand-withdrawal communication is motivated by a desire for greater intimacy and a stronger connection between partners (Christensen & Heavey, 1990). Making demands may also be necessary to bring about change in what are perceived to be inequitable arrangements or to correct power imbalances in a marriage. For example, a study of 494 married couples found that a wife-demand–husband-withdrawal pattern was predicted by wives' dissatisfaction with the division of housework (Kluwer, Heesink, & van de Vliert, 1997). Conversely, Klinetob and Smith (1996) observed that when husbands desire change in the marital relationship, a husband-demand–wife-withdrawal pattern occurs. Further, they found that regardless of whether the wife or husband makes the demands, the vast majority of couples exhibited a bidirectional pattern whereby either partner's withdrawal prompts the other partner's demands. In another study, Roberts (2000) found that, contrary to popular stereotypes, the strongest predictor of wives' marital distress was husbands' hostility, and the strongest predictor of husbands' distress was wives' withdrawal. Both husband-demand–wife-withdrawal and wife-demand–husband-withdrawal communication patterns are associated with concurrent marital dissatisfaction and with declining levels of marital satisfaction over time (Heavey, Christensen, & Malamuth, 1995; Kurdek, 1995; Uebelacker, Courtnage, & Whisman, 2003). In sum, hostile behaviors and distancing behaviors cannot be understood apart from their interactional context, but both "fire and ice" tend to corrode intimate bonds (Roberts, 2000).

A final, but very important aspect of marital processes that merits attention is marital aggression. Unfortunately, the literature on divorce and the literature on family violence are largely disparate. As a result, we generally know very little about different types of marital aggression (e.g., "situational couple violence" vs. a more severe and controlling pattern of "intimate terrorism"; Johnson & Ferraro, 2000), and researchers know even less about how marital violence changes over time or its effects on the likelihood of divorce. DeMaris (2000) reports that "only a handful of studies have explored the link between physical conflict and union disruption" (p. 683).

That said, marital violence is prevalent. Estimates indicate that approximately 2 million women are victims of violence perpetrated by their husbands or other intimate male partners (Johnson & Ferraro, 2000); 22% of women report being victims of physical assault by their male partners, and 9% were beaten up by their partners (U.S. National Institute of Justice, 2000). Men are less likely to be victimized by a partner and less likely to be severely injured by partner violence, but men are more likely than women to be victims of violent resistance (more commonly termed self-defense; Johnson & Ferraro, 2000), and there are indications that this type of violence may be a precursor to a woman leaving her abusive partner (Jacobson & Gottman, 1998). Analyzing the first two waves of the National Survey of Families and Households, DeMaris (2000) found that husbands' physical aggression resulted in diminished marital quality for both partners and significantly increased the likelihood of later marital disruption. Evidence from other studies corroborates the finding that marital aggression is associated with rapid deteriorations in marital satisfaction and a heightened risk of divorce (Lawrence & Bradbury, 2001; Rodrigues et al., 2006; Rogge & Bradbury, 1999; Sanchez & Gager, 2000).

Lawrence, Ro, Barry, and Bunde (2006) proposed a model to explain the mechanisms through which physical aggression leads to relationship distress and dissolution. They suggest that two important behavioral mediators are psychological aggression and emotional disengagement. Acts of psychological aggression are very common in marriage and include behaviors such as threats, coercive tactics, manipulation, verbal harassment, and attempts to annoy or humiliate a partner. Longitudinal research demonstrates that psychological aggression is associated with subsequent declines in relationship satisfaction and victims' personal well-being, as well as an increased likelihood of relationship dissolution (Jacobson et al., 1996; Lawrence et al., 2006).

Emotional disengagement, discussed in greater detail below, is also quite prevalent in marriage and may serve as another mediator of the relationship between physical aggression and relationship dissolution. As conflicts arise and feelings of love, affection, and satisfaction typically decline early in marriage, partners often feel disillusioned with each other and begin to grow apart (Huston & Houts, 1998). Physical aggression occurs with greater frequency and severity early in marriage (Lawrence et al., 2006), and early aggression is probably both a result of partners' disillusionment with each other and a contributor to further emotional distancing. Lawrence et al. suggest that aggressive (or formerly aggressive) individuals lack constructive conflict management skills and thus may avoid disagreements, disengage from conflicts rather than risk the possibility of escalation, or even avoid some situations altogether. As a result, according to this model, couples become disengaged emotionally and behaviorally, undermining relationship quality and increasing the probability of dissolution.

In the next section, we describe the process of marital decline that unfolds as couples begin to grow apart and as partners become more dissatisfied with their relationship and have thoughts about divorce.

\\\\ THE PROCESS OF MARITAL DECLINE

Most spouses care deeply about each other and share strong romantic feelings for one another, at least for a period of time. For some couples, these feelings may endure for many years, perhaps even a lifetime. But for the majority of couples, the strong passionate feelings that contributed to the decision to marry begin to fade in the early years of marriage, feelings of dissatisfaction surface, and a process of emotional disengagement or marital disaffection may be activated. Kayser and Rao (2006) define marital disaffection as "the gradual breaking down of an emotional attachment, a decline in caring about the partner, an emotional estrangement, and a sense of apathy and indifference toward one's spouse" (p. 202).

This process of emotional disengagement is distinct from, but may overlap or coincide with, marital dissatisfaction. Longitudinal studies document that marital satisfaction declines sharply during the first 10 years of marriage (Glenn, 1998), with the steepest decline occurring in the first 2 years (Kurdek, 1998; Lindahl, Clements, & Markman, 1998); after the first decade, there are continuing but more gradual declines throughout the lifetime of the marriage (Vaillant & Vaillant, 1993). Several factors contribute to the downward trajectory for marital satisfaction during the first 2 years of marriage, including diminished feelings of love, declining expressions of affection, and increases in ambivalence and marital conflict (Huston & Houts, 1998). Not surprisingly, research following marriages over time documents a strong link between declining marital dissatisfaction and the odds of becoming divorced or separated (Kim & McKenry, 2002).

It is important to note, however, that although marital disaffection and dissatisfaction are common, they do not always lead to divorce. For a variety of reasons, many couples choose to stay in unhappy marriages. For example, spouses who endorse a belief that marriage is a lifetime commitment, who value the investments they made in a relationship over many years, and who perceive a lack of attractive alternatives are likely to remain in unhappy marriages (Fine, 2000; Heaton & Albrecht, 1991). Further, Hetherington's (2003) longitudinal studies documented that unhappy marriages can be maintained for many years and can take many forms, including the *pursuer-distancer* (or demand-withdraw) relationships described above, *disengaged* marriages in which husbands and wives lead largely parallel lives and have few shared interests or activities, and *operatic* marriages, characterized by frequent quarreling and emotionally volatile interactions.

Understanding that there is a well-established pattern whereby marital satisfaction declines over time for most couples and that dissatisfaction does not always predict divorce, how are researchers to conceptualize the process of marital decline? As we noted earlier in this chapter and will elaborate on in Chapter 6, research suggests that the process is highly variable, it is not linear and continuous, it does not proceed along a uniform trajectory or timetable, and it cannot be characterized by a clearly defined set of sequential stages. Instead, marital breakdown is characterized by discontinuity, peaks and valleys in marital happiness, oscillating periods of marital growth and decline, and often confusing feelings of uncertainty and ambivalence. In a fascinating ethnographic study of newly divorced individuals, Hopper (1993) found that all of his respondents (regardless of whether they considered themselves to be the leaver or the person who was left) reported multiple complaints about the marriage, all were well aware of the problems in their marriages for a long time, and all contemplated divorce at various points throughout the marriage. At the same time, however, they all described good things about their marriages and reasons they wanted to stay in the relationship, creating intense feelings of ambivalence and agonizing decisions about whether and when to divorce.

In addition to the process of marital deterioration being dynamic, fluid, and nonlinear, abundant evidence indicates that the process is a prolonged one that typically unfolds over several years, a process that may begin in the first years of marriage (Huston et al., 2001; Kurdek, 2002) or even during courtship (Huston & Houts, 1998). Kayser and Rao (2006) studied a sample of disaffected married individuals and found that 40% of their respondents experienced their first doubts about their marriage during the first 6 months of their marriage, and another 20% felt their first doubts between 6 months and 1 year.

Kayser and Rao described three phases that couples experience during the process of marital disaffection: beginning disappointments (e.g., disillusionment, attempts to accommodate the partner, keeping silent), escalating anger and hurt (e.g., greater attention to the partner's negative behaviors and traits, inability to see the partner's good traits, and calculation of the costs and benefits of leaving the marriage), and finally, apathy and indifference (feelings of loss, reaching out to friends and family, and taking concrete steps to end the marriage). We do not have empirical information to assess this, but it is likely that couples move through these phases at different rates and that even partners within the same marriage may not experience the same phases of this process in the same way or at the same time. Further, at any one time an individual may confront elements of two or three of the phases (e.g., disillusionment, escalating anger, and apathy and indifference). In other words, the process is best understood as circular, in that individuals likely return to and reexperience feelings, challenges, and coping strategies that they had experienced earlier in the process. Viewed differently, the process represents a dialectical tension between wanting stability-sameness versus change-difference.

Traditionally, researchers have conceptualized divorce, and the process of relationship dissolution more broadly, as progressing through a series of stages (e.g., Lee, 1984), stations (Bohannan, 1968), or phases (e.g., Duck, 1982; Rollie & Duck, 2006). While such models (described in greater detail in Chapter 6) are useful in identifying separate dimensions of a complex and layered process, stage models suggest a more predictable, structured, linear, and irreversible process than what most divorcing individuals actually experience. Generally, scholars have recognized that the stages or phases represent overlapping experiences (Bohannan, 1968), but in using temporal language (such as that one stage follows another) and in describing the resolution of the demands presented in one phase as necessary for successfully entering the next phase, the emphasis of such models is on an ordered, sequential, and generally inevitable progression from one stage to the next. Our view, emphasized throughout this book, is that divorce does not follow such a uniform progression. We turn now to the changing dynamics of parent–child relationships and family members' functioning in the years leading up to divorce.

🕮 PREDISRUPTION PARENT–CHILD PROCESSES

In addition to tension and discord in the marital relationship, predisrupted families in which children are present also exhibit elevated levels of stress and conflict in parent–child relationships. Although only a small number of studies have tracked changes in parent–child interaction through the disruption process, accumulating evidence suggests that over a period of several years prior to divorce, parents are less involved with their children, and they are less effective and less consistent in their parenting. Shaw, Emery, and Tuer (1993) found that, in families on the verge of marital breakup, parents showed less concern for and more rejection of sons. Two panel studies analyzing large nationally representative samples corroborated this pattern. Examining longitudinal data from the Marital Instability Over the Life Course project, Amato and Booth (1996) found that in comparison to parents who remained married over the course of the study, parents who would later divorce reported more problems with their adolescents, a greater likelihood of being abusive to their children, and less satisfaction with their spouses' relationships with the children as early as 8 to 12 years prior to divorce. Similarly, Sun (2001) analyzed data from the National Educational Longitudinal Study (NELS) and observed that, compared with adolescents whose parents did not subsequently divorce, those in predivorce families reported more distant relationships with their parents, lower levels of interaction and fewer discussions with parents, and less parental involvement in their educational activities. In addition, parents reported lower expectations for their children's educational attainment.

The nature of individual family members' functioning is another salient dimension of the predivorce family environment. During the often long period leading up to separation and divorce, children, adolescents, and adults exhibit more behavior problems and lower levels of well-being than their counterparts in families that do not experience divorce. Block, Block, and Gjerde (1986) found that boys whose parents would later divorce were more anxious, aggressive, impulsive, and disobedient as much as 11 years prior to parental divorce. Similarly, Doherty and Needle (1991) observed that levels of psychological problems and substance abuse were elevated among girls prior to divorce, and a longitudinal analysis of children in Great Britain and the United States documented that children whose parents later divorced had elevated levels of behavior problems, diminished academic achievement, and frequent exposure to marital conflict (Cherlin et al., 1991). Sun's (2001) research found that, even controlling for relevant demographic variables, both boys and girls from predivorce families exhibited more behavior problems and deficits in academic performance, self-esteem, locus of control, and educational aspirations compared with their peers in families in which parents remained married.

Adults whose marriages are deteriorating and who are often simultaneously struggling with other problems such as neuroticism, antisocial behavior, or alcohol or drug use can be expected to be less effective and consistent in their parenting (Hetherington & Kelly, 2002). Clearly, these processes are reciprocal and interdependent. Marital decline, ineffective parenting, child maladjustment, and compromised parental well-being are common characteristics of predivorce families, and each of these processes can be viewed as being both a product of and a contributor to the other processes. For example, child maladjustment and difficulties in parent–child relationships are strong predictors of parental maladjustment (Kent & Peplar, 2003; Rubin & Burgess, 2002). Further, during the period leading up to separation and divorce, families typically experience a downward trajectory in social mobility that exacerbates preexisting family tensions and behavior problems (Morrison & Cherlin, 1995).

❧ CONCLUSIONS

It is not the case that all marriages begin with equal chances of success. Macrostructural arrangements (see Chapter 4) create contexts in which some marriages have greater resources and fewer stressors than other marriages. Sociodemographic and life-course variables such as socioeconomic status, race, early age at marriage, and premarital childbearing can be viewed as distal factors affecting the probability of divorce. Personality characteristics and behavior problems that individuals bring to marriage represent more proximal causes of divorce. Marital relationship processes that undermine marital satisfaction and heighten the chances of divorce include infidelity, poor communication, a demand-withdrawal pattern, and psychological and physical aggression.

For many couples, the process of marital decline and disaffection is initiated early in the marriage as partners begin to feel disillusioned with each other and disappointed in their relationship. We emphasize that the pathways to divorce are not as linear, predictable, and sequential as earlier models may have led us to think; instead, trajectories of marital decline are fluid, discontinuous, ambiguous, and highly variable. And perhaps as important, marital decline affects not only the couple, but many other subsystems in the family. In Chapter 6, we turn our attention to processes surrounding and following couples' decision to separate, and we highlight variations in the uncoupling process.

6

Variations in Separation and Uncoupling

Stephanie Rollie

Describing divorce as a process, as opposed to an event, points to the complex and varied nature of marital uncoupling (Duck, 1982). It recognizes that separating lives and households takes time. The divorce process is multifaceted and often involves changes in multiple areas of one's life, including household structure, personal identity, daily routines, social networks, and financial resources. It is fraught with uncertainty, ambiguity, and unpredictability, and although divorce may be considered a normalized process in many cultures, the experience of divorce is rarely "normal" for those going through it.

At the same time, describing divorce as a process can be problematic. It can bring to mind a series of linear steps or stages that individuals march though in the changing of their status from married to divorced. Indeed, the notion of divorce as a process has been the basis for many models developed to delineate and describe the common progression associated with divorce and relational breakup (e.g., Bohannan, 1968; Lee, 1984). These models denote the typical development of divorce as described by individuals who retrospectively structure and make sense of their experiences—that is, an important factor contributing to the development of stage models is the set of methods that researchers have used to examine the divorce process. By the time they are interviewed, most divorced individuals have "made sense" of what happened, and they have developed elaborate accounts of their breakups that, by definition, filter out much of the ambiguity, inconsistency, contradiction, and uncertainty that they experienced during the divorce process (Hopper, 1993; Rollie & Duck, 2006). Thus, the retrospective stories that researchers hear paint a more ordered, predetermined, and stage-like process than the stories they might hear if divorcing individuals were interviewed in the moment when feelings of anger, hurt, and chaos are salient and before social support is mobilized.

Divorce is neither linear nor a series of predictable events. There is no one divorce process that can begin to capture the widely varied day-to-day experiences of marital uncoupling. As we argue throughout the book, marital uncoupling is fluid, dynamic, and varied. In this sense, it is useful to think about the divorce experience as multiple processes that may be sequential, simultaneous, circular, interconnected, or separate depending on each individual's unique circumstances (Rollie & Duck, 2006).

This chapter focuses on variations in separation and divorce experiences. As we address the divorce process, we are referring to the wide-ranging paths, trajectories, experiences, and emotions associated with marital uncoupling. It is the culmination of these experiences that individuals often refer to as "the divorce," but the divorce process may begin long before separation and continue long after the legal divorce is finalized. We begin by examining the multiple and varied processes associated with the divorce experience. We then describe specific points of variation that have been identified as important in shaping an individual's specific divorce experiences. Next, we point to variations in postdivorce processes. Finally, although research on the uncoupling process itself tends to focus on the experiences of the adults, the process of divorce often involves children as well. Accordingly, we finish this chapter by briefly discussing the inclusion of children in scholarly work on the separation process.

❧ SEPARATION AS MULTIPLE PROCESSES

Bohannan's (1968) early work depicting the six stations of divorce illustrates the multiple processes associated with marital uncoupling. Bohannan argued that individuals move through or experience six different *stations* in the process of divorce. These include a) the emotional divorce, in which couples grow apart and one or both individuals determine that the relationship is no longer viable; b) the legal divorce, which includes the legal proceedings and processes associated with the termination of the marriage contract; c) the economic divorce, which involves the division of joint property and assets; d) the coparental divorce, which involves the determination of legal and physical custody of children; e) the community divorce, in which the social network is restructured; and f) the psychic divorce, in which each individual psychologically separates him- or herself from the marriage and develops an autonomous self.

Although these stations were originally characterized as a sequence of experiences that individuals move through as they divorce, we suggest that each station can be characterized as one of the many processes that occur (often simultaneously) during marital uncoupling—that is, the legal and economic processes are interconnected with, and yet distinct from, emotional and psychic processes, coparental processes, and community processes. Some processes may occur at the same time as others, or processes may unfold sequentially. Some may last only a short time, while others may continue long after the legal uncoupling is complete. The experience of each process varies from couple to couple, even person to person, and is influenced by a number of factors (e.g., length of marriage, presence of children, the individual's and the partner's emotional and psychological attachment to each other). Accordingly, knowledge of the divorce experience emerges from understanding the unique combination of processes and associated experiences for each individual.

Hagestad and Smyer (1982) further depict the complexity of the divorce process. Specifically, they describe three types of losses that individuals manage during and following marital termination that can greatly impact their divorce experience. First, individuals experience the loss of emotional attachments. Particularly when one person does not want to end the relationship, the loss of emotional attachments to both the spouse and the family unit can be traumatic. Individuals may feel that they are losing their family or their best friend and must find ways to cope with these losses. They may find themselves managing an assortment of competing emotions, including guilt, frustration, anger, and relief. Individuals often deal with feelings of failure associated with dissolution of the marriage, in addition to the many changes divorce necessitates.

A second loss experienced by divorcing individuals is an inability to perform valued roles. During the divorce process, individuals must come to terms with the notion that they can no longer assume the role of wife or husband. In this sense, individuals may feel that they have lost a core part of their identity, particularly if the spousal role was valued. When children are involved, the divorce usually brings about a division of households, a division that affects the parental role as well. Individuals find that they can no longer enact the parental role in the same way without the presence of the other spouse and that the two-household structure constrains one's ability to parent when children are staying with the other parent (Rollie, 2006). Additionally, as social networks change during the divorce process, individuals may lose other valued roles, such as aunt or uncle, sister- or brother-in-law, son- or daughter-in-law, and even some friend roles. Thus, part of the divorce process involves coming to terms with the many ways that one's sense of self is altered through changes in relationships and roles.

A third process identified by Hagestad and Smyer (1982) that individuals negotiate during divorce is the loss of routines and rituals. During the marriage, spouses and families develop taken-for-granted patterns of interaction. These patterns provide structure and shape day-to-day functioning. They may include processes for eating dinner as a family, bedtime rituals, television viewing, and even end-of-day debriefings. Often, individuals do not realize the value of these basic rituals and routines until they can no longer be enacted. As a result, individuals may feel that they no longer know how to function in the world as well as they previously did. They must cope with losing valued routines while working to develop new routines and rituals, some of which may now be performed alone or in a new location.

Duck's (2005; Rollie & Duck, 2006) model of relationship dissolution similarly focuses on multiple processes associated with relationship termination. Each process denotes distinct and identifiable patterns of communication and behavior. Specifically, Duck suggests that relational uncoupling involves five processes. Intrapsychic processes occur when individuals reflect on their relationship and their partner's behavior in relation to expectations about equity and desired outcomes. Individuals may evaluate their satisfaction in the relationship based on an examination of costs, rewards, and relational alternatives (Rusbult & Buunk, 1993). For this process, individuals may decide that they are unhappy and want to seek change or that they are willing to continue as things are. In some cases, a person may decide to alter his or her own behavior or expectations to achieve a desired relational state.

Dyadic processes involve "relational talks" that focus on the current status and future of the relationship. Members may discuss reasons for staying in the relationship as well as reasons for ending the relationship. These talks may end in reconciliation or dissolution, or they may end ambiguously when individuals do not know what will happen with the relationship. Dyadic processes may occur over and over in a circular fashion until one or both people determine that the relationship cannot be salvaged and that termination is either inevitable or the best outcome.

Engagement in social (support) processes moves relational talk outside of the relationship to the social network as individuals negotiate relational meanings with friends and family. Individuals may seek advice, develop accounts of relational problems, seek support, and provide updates on the status of the relationship. In grave-dressing processes, individuals construct summary stories or accounts of the relationship and the reasons for its outcome in line with cultural scripts. Different accounts may be developed for different audiences. In laying the relationship to rest, individuals work to construct and present a self that is still relationally desirable. Finally, in resurrection processes, individuals prepare for the future. They recognize that they have been shaped by their experiences in the previous relationship, which will, in turn, affect engagement in future relationships. Again, these processes are not necessarily linear, and each is filled with potentially unlimited variation.

The three sets of processes described here (Bohannan, 1968; Duck, 2005; Hagestad & Smyer, 1982) point to the multifaceted nature of what is often simply called "divorce." It becomes clear upon examining these processes that the boundaries of divorce are rather fuzzy. As discussed earlier in this book (see Chapter 2), for some the divorce process can begin long before any legal proceedings or even dyadic discussions about the desire for a divorce take place. Similarly, some continue to manage divorce processes associated with loss and the psychic divorce years after the legal proceedings have been completed. Marital partners often move through and experience the processes very differently. One person may have already moved on before the other even knows that divorce proceedings are on the horizon. Thus, to study and understand divorce, it is important to identify and recognize the multiple layers of the divorce experience. It is not a linear progression of steps and stages depicted through the summary of retellings of divorce experiences. Instead, the experience of divorce involves multiple, overlapping, but discernible processes. The engagement and management of these different processes ultimately shape family members' divorce experiences.

\\\ POINTS OF VARIATION IN THE DIVORCE PROCESS

Baxter's (1984) exploration of the trajectories of relationship disengagement illustrates nicely the complexity and variation associated with marital uncoupling. Using 92 accounts of nonmarital romantic relationship breakups, Baxter sought to delineate basic patterns and paths (as opposed to a singular process) of relationship termination. The results included a complex flowchart (see Figure 6.1) of disengagement that focuses on six critical features or points in the breakup process. These include 1) whether the onset of relational problems is gradual or sudden, 2) whether one or both individuals desire to end the relationship, 3) the use of indirect or direct strategies to terminate the relationship, 4) the speed and extent of disengagement negotiation, 5) whether attempts are made to repair the relationship, and 6) whether the relationship is terminated or continued in some (current or other) form. Each of these critical features characterizes points of variation in the breakup process. Interestingly, many of the critical features identified by Baxter correspond with what other researchers have identified as significant points in the divorce process. Some of these will be further discussed later in this section.

The flowchart depicts potential disengagement trajectories and illustrates the complexity of the negotiation to terminate a relationship. The first step of the flowchart is the onset of relationship problems. This is the point at which the separating process begins. Baxter describes two paths that lead relationships to this point: *incrementalism* and *critical incident*. Incrementalism describes the gradual buildup of relational issues and problems until a particular threshold is reached and one or both individuals determine that the relationship is either no longer desirable or no longer viable. In contrast, a critical incident refers to one egregious act, problem, or experience (e.g., infidelity) that propels the relationship into decline. Although incrementalism occurs over time (at least for one member), the critical incident occurs with little warning. This leads to the second step, the decision to exit the relationship, which occurs in one of two ways: unilaterally, in which one person wants to terminate the relationship, or bilaterally, in which the decision is mutual. It is at this point that the flowchart diverges into two distinct paths, thus indicating that the negotiation and experiences of relationship dissolution are different, depending on how the process is started.

Steps 3 to 5 are associated with the unilateral dissolution process and Steps 6 and 7 are associated with the bilateral process. The unilateral process begins with initiating unilateral dissolution actions. In this step, Baxter delineates the different ways that an individual may communicate the desire to terminate the relationship. Specifically, strategies differ based on the level of directness employed by the individual. Some relational partners directly indicate their dissatisfaction using a *fait accompli* style,

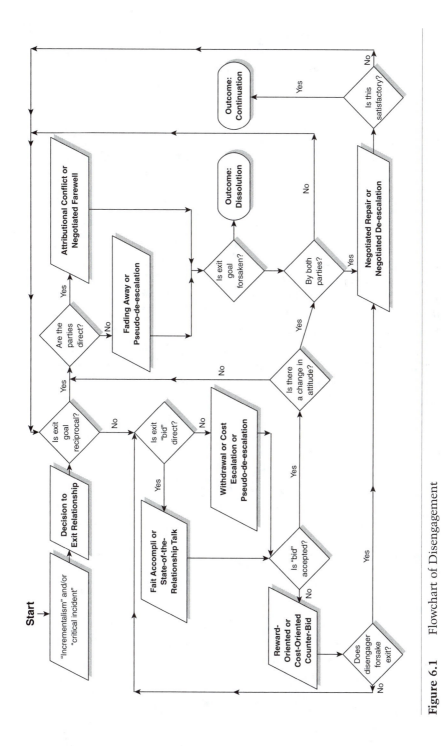

Figure 6.1 Flowchart of Disengagement

Source: Reprinted from Baxter, L. A. (1984). Trajectories of relationship disengagement. *Journal of Social and Personal Relationships, 1,* 29–48.

in which the person declares that the relationship is over with no opportunity for discussion, or state-of-the-relationship talk, in which the person presents relational problems and invites dyadic discussion about the issue. Alternatively, some individuals are more indirect, using withdrawal, which involves letting the relationship wither away by avoiding the other; pseudo-de-escalation, which involves transforming the relationship and reducing intimacy (e.g., to friendship) without indicating the intention to terminate the relationship; or cost escalation, which involves intentionally behaving in ways that will lead the other person to terminate the relationship.

Steps 4 and 5, the initial reaction of the broken-up party and ambivalence and repair scenarios, both focus on how the news of the desire to terminate the relationship is received and addressed. Upon receiving the news or recognizing the partner's desire to end the relationship, an individual may accept or resist the bid. Cost-oriented (e.g., threats or enacted sanctions against the partner) or reward-oriented resistance (e.g., promise of positive behavior or outcomes) necessitates a response from the person expressing the desire to terminate. The disengager may reinforce the desire to end the relationship or may reconsider. If the latter occurs, relational partners may negotiate relational repair in which the relationship is restored or negotiate de-escalation in which the relationship is transformed into another form (e.g., friendship).

Step 6, initiating bilateral dissolution action, occurs indirectly through fading away when the relationship simply ends without any discussion or acknowledgment or through pseudo-de-escalation in which both parties suggest transforming the relationship when both really intend to terminate the relationship. Alternatively, it may occur directly through negotiated farewell, in which both people discuss the move to terminate, or attributional conflict, which adds an element of hostility through assignment of blame. This leads to Step 7, ambivalence and repair scenarios, in which, similar to Step 5, partners may choose to repair or terminate the relationship. Couples—and the partners within them—may find themselves making multiple passes through the model as they negotiate the meaning of problems and issues, their desire to remain in the relationship, and their desire to leave.

Baxter's model illustrates the wide range of dissolution paths and experiences associated with the dissolution experience. Variation exists along each dimension: how the decision to terminate the relationship emerges; the extent to which one or both people want to leave or remain in the relationship; the wide range of strategies used to terminate, resist, or repair the relationship; the extent of negotiation before a decision is reached; and the result of the negotiation as continuation or dissolution. Baxter acknowledged in her discussion that some of the categories in the flowchart are overly simplistic and do not capture the true variety of strategies and processes of negotiation described by participants. Although her research was based on nonmarital romantic relationships, most of these processes also apply to marital termination; in fact, many of these processes may be even more significant and complicated in marital relationships given the increased levels of commitment and investment often associated with marriage. The remainder of this section further describes specific points of variation in the divorce process identified by researchers.

The decision to separate. The decision to separate is an important component of the divorce process. The emotional divorce (Bohannan, 1968), intrapsychic processes (Duck, 1982, 2005), and the gradual versus sudden onset of problems (Baxter, 1984) described above all focus on the ways that an individual or couple comes to the point of initiating the legal divorce. The decision to separate can be an extremely complex, difficult, and emotional process. It can occur quite quickly, as in the case of an egregious act, or may be reached only after years of assessing and weighing costs, rewards, and alternatives (Levinger, 1979). Often, the decision is based on a number of factors, many of which are tied to stress within and outside of the marriage (Bodenmann et al., 2007). The decision to separate often involves engaging in multiple processes of sense making until one or both individuals reach a point that a divorce seems to be the only logical option (Willén & Montgomery, 2006).

For some, doubts about the relationship begin shortly after getting married, as individuals experience disillusionment with their partner and the marriage (Kayser & Rao, 2006). Some individuals complain that their partners do not behave as they had expected or that the partners have substantially "changed." Behaviors that were once viewed positively start to be perceived as significant flaws (Femlee, 1995). As the marriage continues, disillusionment can turn to anger and hurt and finally apathy and indifference (Kayser & Rao, 2006). This process of marital disaffection, in which feelings of affection and love dissipate over time, leads many individuals to seriously contemplate terminating the relationship. Spouses may give up hope that they can change their partner or the relationship for the better and reach a point of having to determine whether to stay in an unhappy marriage or to push for dissolution.

The decision to divorce often involves both an individual and a dyadic component (Duck, 1982, 2005; Rollie & Duck, 2006)—that is, as in the process of marital disaffection, an individual may grapple with whether or not to seek a divorce long before presenting the possibility or desire to his or her spouse. At the dyadic level, a couple may debate and negotiate various options and alternatives before one or both ultimately begin the legal process. Even once the legal divorce is in motion, couples may repair and reconnect, only to begin the process again months or years later. The complicated and cyclical nature of the decision to separate is illustrated in Battaglia, Richard, Datteri, and Lord's (1998) ordered script of relationship dissolution. Using 74 step-by-step accounts of breakup, they identified 16 general steps that form the cultural script of breakup: 1) have a lack of interest, 2) notice other people, 3) act distant, 4) try to work things out, 5) are physically distant-avoidant, 6) have a lack of interest, 7) consider breaking up, 8) communicate feelings, 9) try to work things out, 10) notice other people, 11) act distant, 12) date other people, 13) get back together, 14) consider breaking up, 15) move on and recover, and 16) break up. This breakup script suggests that individuals cycle between cognitive and interactive processes before reaching a final decision to terminate the relationship. The nature, extent, and sequence of individual and dyadic processes vary from relationship to relationship.

Willén and Montgomery (2006) describe a variety of strategies that individuals employ in wrestling with the decision to divorce. They argue that spouses engage in cognitive processes or interactional behaviors that help them to stave off the decision to terminate the relationship, to feel like the decision is necessary and justified, or to prepare for the inevitable outcome. In making efforts to keep the relationship going, spouses report focusing on the good parts of the relationship and de-emphasizing the significance of negative events in the hope that the relationship or their feelings about the relationship might improve. Some spouses also deflect dissatisfaction by increasing their investments in the relationship (e.g., having a baby or buying a house).

To justify and make sense out of marital dissatisfaction and their desire to terminate the relationship, spouses sometimes inflate the importance of negative events or behaviors, point to an inability to change or rectify the situation, and blame and criticize the other spouse. In line with Baxter's cost-escalation, Willén and Montgomery also found that individuals reported provoking and inciting their partner so that he or she would make the decision to terminate the relationship. Individuals may employ strategies that help them prepare for the divorce by mentally fantasizing about alternative possibilities, emotionally distancing themselves from their spouse, exploring alternative relationships, investigating practical solutions and arrangements for postdivorce living, and nurturing a separate and independent self. Thus, an important part of the decision process is the need to conclude that the divorce is justifiable and to be able to present oneself as a responsible person.

Initiating and "being left." Separating spouses experience the divorce in different ways. Variation in divorce experiences is evident when comparing those who initiate the divorce with those "being left" (Buehler, 1987; Hopper, 1993, 2001). Divorcing spouses often have little difficulty identifying the person who initiated the divorce based on who made the final decision to end the marriage (Hopper, 1993). However, it is not always clear who the real initiator is. The person who emotionally disengages from the relationship is not always the person who initiates the physical separation or the legal divorce proceedings (Hewitt, Western, & Baxter, 2006; Vannoy, 2000). Similarly, the person who initiates legal proceedings is not necessarily the person who makes the final decision to end the marriage (Hopper, 1993). Sometimes individuals are manipulated into filing for divorce, for example, if the spouse has emotionally left or has an alternative romantic relationship outside of the marriage (Rokach, Cohen, & Dreman, 2004). As the ones often responsible for monitoring the quality of the relationship and how it is affecting family members, wives sometimes initiate separation because they want to protect their children from a troubled marriage or because they know that their husband is unhappy with the marriage (Hewitt et al., 2006). In other cases, both individuals may be equally unhappy with the marriage and desire termination, but one person finally initiates the separation and divorce processes (Hopper, 1993).

At the same time, the process of labeling oneself as the leaver or the person who has been left can differently shape the divorce experience. The process of changing one's identity, the type of account given for why the divorce occurred, feelings about the divorce, and the rate at which individuals move on are some of the ways that initiators and noninitiators differ in their descriptions of and reactions to divorce. For example, initiators and noninitiators make sense of and account for their divorce differently (Harvey & Fine, 2006; Hopper, 1993, 2001). Initiators often assign responsibility for ending the marriage to those outside of the marriage (Hopper, 2001). As a result, they often describe the marriage as not being real or as being fundamentally flawed from the beginning (Hopper, 2001). They also tend to focus more on specific problems during or before the marriage that would justify termination (Hopper, 1993). Noninitiators, on the other hand, are more likely to convey that they were manipulated and lied to by their spouses and that they did not want the divorce (Hopper, 1993, 2001). Thus, the process of justifying the divorce, describing their role in the divorce decision, and preserving a sense of self to outsiders is different for spouses, depending on how they perceive their role in the dissolution process, even if they felt (and currently feel) similarly about the need for a divorce.

The process of moving from a married role to a divorced or single role is also different for initiators and noninitiators (Duran-Aydintug, 1995). Initiators may begin with secret doubts and dissatisfaction with the marriage. They often have fears regarding how their spouses and family members might react to their desire to terminate the relationship. In getting ready, initiators confide in friends and family while simultaneously distancing themselves from the spousal role. As they receive social support, their doubts about the marriage are reinforced and initiators feel bolstered in confronting their spouse. As initiators go public, they try out their new single roles. They feel in control and anticipate their new life. Finally, in the old-new me processes, initiators manage their new identities by changing their appearance, forming new friendship networks, and presenting themselves as single.

The divorce experience can be very different for noninitators. Many initially experience shock and disbelief. If they truly are surprised by the initiation of divorce proceedings by their partner, they are often hurt and feel helpless upon hearing the news of their spouse's desire to end the relationship. Noninitiators often remain committed to their spouse and to the marriage and work to make the changes necessary to save the relationship and preserve their spousal role (trial processes). As the legal divorce process moves forward, noninitiators describe themselves as reacting. They simply follow along as the initiator moves through the logistics associated with the legal divorce. Finally, noninitators describe themselves as on the bridge. They struggle to make sense out of the failure of the marriage. They are often still tied to the spousal role and identify themselves as an ex-spouse.

Levels of control and awareness of what is happening significantly influence the process (Duran-Aydintug, 1995; Thuen & Rice, 2006). Because they have already moved through periods of doubt and have made peace with the decision, initiators are able to look toward and prepare for the future. Noninitiators, on the other hand, are often surprised by the news and struggle to make sense of what is happening. For them, it is unclear what the final outcome might be or look like. As a result, it can take much longer to recover from the divorce and to move on to a future outside of the marriage (Sakraida, 2005). Throughout the process, noninitiators may hold on to the hope that the relationship may still be saved and actively or passively resist the other's bid(s) to end the relationship. By ignoring the other's provocations, pretending to agree with the divorce, and being impassive and nonresponsive to the request, noninitiators work to preserve their spousal role (Willén & Montgomery, 2006).

Another factor that significantly contributes to different experiences for initiators and noninitiators is the presence of an alternative relationship (Rokach et al., 2004). This new relationship becomes an additional source of support and, as the better alternative to the marriage, helps individuals construct a new life outside of the marriage. Identity strength may play a role as well—that is, individuals with more moral worth (i.e., higher levels of self-respect, honesty, and trustworthiness), unity (continuity of self over time), autonomy, and self-determination are more likely to wish to save their marriages than to initiate separation (Vannoy, 2000). In short, the experience of divorce can be dramatically different for each spouse, even if each similarly desires to end the relationship. These differences are often manifested in the ways that individuals talk about the divorce process, their ex-spouse, and themselves.

Social networks and support. Duck (1982, 2005) and Bohannan (1968) both describe processes associated with divorce that involve individuals outside of the marital relationship, specifically friends, family, and other members of the social network. Divorcing individuals turn to members of their social network, who, in turn, can affect divorce processes. Friends and family may directly or indirectly impact the progression of the divorce (Duran-Aydintug, 1995; Sprecher, Felmlee, Schmeeckle, & Shu, 2006). For example, an important part of the divorce process is the need to present oneself as a responsible person (Willén & Montgomery, 2006). Whether family and friends approve of a divorce can be an important consideration for married individuals (Knoester & Booth, 2000). When members of the social network support the divorce, they may actually encourage a person to initiate physical separation or legal proceedings. Conversely, when friends and family members convey that a divorce is not appropriate or necessary, the social network may act to discourage initiation.

Additionally, as individuals move through divorce processes, the attitudes of members of the social network can influence both the experience of and adjustment following divorce (Kunz & Kunz, 1995). It is generally agreed upon that divorce is a stressful period; in fact, the primary piece of advice that some individuals give to those considering divorce is not to do it (Knox & Corte, 2007). Thus, to help manage the stress and one's identity, many individuals turn to members of their social network for advice, support, someone to listen, and social interaction at various points on the divorce trajectory (Kunz & Kunz, 1995; Smerglia, Miller, & Kort-Butler, 1999). Individuals also gain support through joining organizations or clubs (Kunz & Kunz, 1995). In short, individuals vary in the extent to which they turn to members of their social network for support and advice, the extent to which they are supported by those members, and the impact that social support has on both the individual and the divorce process.

Network reorganization following divorce. During divorce, most individuals experience changes in their social networks in terms of the size of the network, type of network members, and levels of closeness (Albeck & Kaydar, 2002; Terhell, Broese van Groenou, & van Tilburg, 2004). These social networks may include friends, kin, in-laws, colleagues, neighbors, and others. Network restructuring processes may begin early in marital decline as individuals confide in friends and family about their dissatisfaction, frustration, and concerns with the marriage. In offering support to one spouse, network members may intentionally or inadvertently pull away from the other. This begins to set the stage for network reorganization as the divorce moves forward.

During the marriage, individuals' networks often merge and overlap as in-laws, each spouse's friends, and other new friends are gained (Sprecher et al., 2006). During the divorce, many of these relationships return to their status before the marriage—that is, each spouse generally retains relationships with his or her premarital family and friends (Albeck & Kaydar, 2002). Relationships with close friends and family members may be strengthened as divorcing individuals call upon them for support. In contrast, contact with couple friends developed during the marriage often declines following the divorce, and contact with in-laws diminishes. The social network typically declines in size during and directly following divorce. Individuals vary in the extent to which they build back up their social network (Terhell et al., 2004). As divorce processes subside, some women expand their social network to include individuals (typically unmarried women) they have met from work, the neighborhood, and organizations to which they belong (Albeck & Kaydar, 2002; Kunz & Kunz, 1995). These individuals appear to experience a type of social liberation in which they embrace their single status and accompanying activities (e.g., bars, dates) (Terhell et al., 2004). Other factors may influence changes in network structure, such as initiator-noninitiator status, gender, and presence of children. For example, initiators may expand their social networks more quickly and engage in more social activities than noninitiators (Thuen & Eikeland, 1998).

CHILDREN'S INVOLVEMENT IN THE SEPARATING PROCESS

Research on the processes associated with marital uncoupling typically focus on spousal experiences and corresponding outcomes for adults and children. It is important to note, however, that children directly or indirectly experience the parental separating processes as well. Sometimes they are directly involved through disclosure of the divorce, talk about the divorce or the other parent, or involvement in decisions relating to the divorce. Children also experience the divorce process indirectly by observing interaction (or lack thereof) between parents. During this time, children are also trying to make sense of the process and the potential implications for themselves and their family in the future. Here, we describe variations in children's involvement in the divorce process by focusing on several time points or processes in which they are often involved.

First, the way that the impending divorce is disclosed to children has been identified by researchers and clinicians as a critical point in the divorce process for both children and parents. Who tells the children, the content of the information, and the manner in which it is conveyed influence how children make sense of the divorce and can ultimately influence children's adjustment (Westberg, Nelson, & Piercy, 2002). Children report that learning about their parents' divorce was a particularly memorable experience. As adults, many can recall exactly when and how they learned about the divorce (Harvey & Fine, 2004; Thomas, Booth-Butterfield, & Booth-Butterfield, 1995). As we discuss in Chapter 8, children's reactions to the news of the divorce are also varied. Some children express relief at hearing the news, particularly when parental conflict prior to separation was high (Cushman & Cahn, 1986; Westberg et al., 2002). Many children experience a mix of emotions including sadness, confusion, worry, anger, and surprise (Ducibella, 1995; Stewart, Copeland, Chester, Malley, & Barenbaum, 1997).

Parents often use a variety of techniques to inform their children about the divorce, often making excuses or offering justifications to children about why the divorce is occurring (Cushman & Cahn, 1986). Parents are not always forthright and honest about the divorce process, perhaps because they may want to protect their children or may feel guilty about the divorce. However, the perception that they were deceived about the divorce can negatively affect children's self-esteem and children's satisfaction with communication with their mothers (Thomas et al., 1995). Although the news typically comes from the mother, sometimes the father or both parents are involved in sharing information about the divorce (Cushman & Cahn, 1986; Westberg et al., 2002). Children often report, however, that they would have preferred to have had both parents involved in conveying the information (Westberg et al., 2002). Additionally, parents do not always disclose information about the divorce to all of the children at the same time or in the same manner. Sometimes, older children receive the news earlier and more informally than younger children (Westberg et al., 2002).

There is also variation in the amount of information shared with children and their level of inclusion in decision making during the divorce process. Providing children with information about the divorce process helps to reduce their uncertainty, and children often indicate that they wish they had more information about what was happening (Thomas et al., 1995). The process of sharing information during the divorce process can even strengthen residential parent–child relationships (Arditti, 1999). However, parents may also disclose information about the divorce or the other spouse that is considered inappropriate and makes children feel uncomfortable (Afifi, 2003). Specifically, in trying to cope with the divorce, parents may say negative things about the other parent, disclose personal concerns, convey financial issues, or relay other information that may be overly sensitive (Afifi, 2003; Koerner, Jacobs, & Raymond, 2002). Parents are more likely to inappropriately disclose information about the divorce when they perceive a lack of control over divorce stressors (Afifi, 2003; Afifi, McManus, Hutchinson, & Baker, 2007). As a result, children can feel "caught in the middle" of their parents' divorce and find themselves acting as a peer, mediator, or counselor (Afifi, 2003; Harvey & Fine, 2004). Additionally, parents vary in the degree to which they include children in the decision-making and negotiation processes associated with where they will live, custody arrangements, and levels of contact with parents (Moxnes, 2003), with older children and adolescents tending to be more involved in such decisions. Accordingly, when they are not consulted or otherwise involved, children can feel left out of the process.

Children also experience the marital separation process through changes in parenting and family practices. This marital disruption process may begin prior to and continue long after the legal divorce (Chase-Lansdale & Hetherington, 1990). During this time, many parents become distressed, which, in turn, affects their parenting behavior (Braver et al., 2006; Morrison & Cherlin, 1995; Wallerstein & Kelly, 1980). This is particularly true when one parent temporarily or permanently moves out of the household and children no longer have regular contact with both parents (Ducibella, 1995; Scott, Booth, King, & Johnson, 2007). Daily routines such as meal- and bedtimes may be altered or disrupted, and parents may engage in less discipline, may spend less time playing with their children, and may have less energy to help with homework (Sun & Li, 2002). Daily patterns and routines may be altered as well when parents suffer a decline in economic resources (Sayer, 2006; Sun & Li, 2002). Sometimes children are introduced to one or both parents' new significant others who could become future stepparents, thus further altering family structure and routines (Moxnes, 2003). These changes can affect children in a variety of ways, and children differ in the ways that they cope with the effects of marital changes (Sun & Li, 2002).

Children experience the divorce process in a myriad of ways. Much research on the involvement of children in marital uncoupling tends to focus on specific outcomes (e.g., psychological, behavioral) for children following the divorce. These outcomes will be discussed further in Chapter 8. Less research focuses on the actual experience of parental divorce for children and the ways they may become involved or excluded from the parents' divorce processes. Additionally, more research should examine the various ways that children experience the multiple divorce processes described above (e.g., changes in social networks, shifts in parental identity).

〰 CONCLUSIONS

The purpose of this chapter is to illustrate the many variations in and fluidity of the separation and divorce process. One of the main points of this chapter is that there are limitations inherent in referring to divorce as a singular process with a definite beginning and end. We suggest that it may be more accurate to think of divorce as consisting of multiple processes, some of which begin long before physical separation or legal proceedings, and some of which unfold for years after one becomes an ex-spouse. For some divorcing couples, the processes may be interconnected and offer similar experiences and outcomes, whereas others may move through these processes in considerably different ways, at different times, and in different sequences. Thus, in understanding and examining the multiple processes described in this chapter, one can begin to understand the true complexity of divorce. Unfortunately, methodological challenges have prevented many studies from capturing the nuances of this process. In the next two chapters, we will discuss variations in the outcomes of these different processes for adults (Chapter 7) and children (Chapter 8).

7

Variation and Fluidity in Adult Adjustment to Divorce

Physical separation and legal divorce are emotionally charged events that evoke a range of positive and negative reactions. On one hand, couples typically separate before legal dissolution, and the separation provides a sense of closure and relief. On the other hand, experiences such as living alone, heading a single-parent household, and becoming a nonresidential parent generate feelings of sadness, guilt, shame, loneliness, and distress. In this chapter, we describe the nature, magnitude, and sources of variation in how adults adjust to divorce. We concentrate on aspects of social and emotional adjustment, which have received the bulk of research attention, but we also address variation in financial adjustment, relationships between former spouses, and coparenting arrangements. Our intent is to explore the two related themes outlined earlier: variability in adults' adjustment to divorce, particularly variation associated with gender and race, and fluidity in adjustment, or changes over time, both of which are highlighted in the box at the far right side of Figure 2.1. We begin by summarizing how marital dissolution impacts adults' social and emotional adjustment, and then we examine their financial adjustment, relations between former spouses, and coparenting arrangements.

⑊ SOCIAL AND EMOTIONAL ADJUSTMENT

It is well established that the psychological well-being of the divorced is worse than that of the married, with divorced adults exhibiting higher rates of unhappiness, depression, distress, and alcohol and substance abuse (Aseltine & Kessler, 1993; Davies, Avison, & McAlpine, 1997; Demo & Acock, 1996a; Horwitz, White, & Howell-White, 1996; Johnson & Wu, 2002; Kim & McKenry, 2002; Marks, 1996; Ross, 1995; Simon & Marcussen, 1999). In a longitudinal study, Horwitz et al. observed that adults who divorced over a 7-year period exhibited nearly twice the number of depressive symptoms and 4 times more alcohol problems than the continuously married. Aseltine and Kessler found that the aggregate effect of marital disruption on depression during the first 3 years following divorce was equal to approximately one fourth of a standard deviation, or comparable to the effects of other major life stressors. Accepting the diminished well-being of the divorced as a general pattern, how much variation is there and what factors are associated with this variation? Why do some adults recover quickly and fare quite well emotionally, while others suffer prolonged depression or neurotic, self-defeating behavior? We begin by examining the personal accounts constructed by recently divorced adults, and we describe the role that personal accounts play in facilitating adjustment to divorce.

Account Making and Narratives

As discussed earlier (in Chapters 2 and 6), the development of a personal narrative or story is a crucial marker on the road to recovery. Constructing an account helps the divorced individual to begin to make sense of what happened and to impose meaning on confusing marital events. Integrating self-reflections into a story facilitates the ability to assess one's own role in the divorce, to attribute responsibility for one's own and others' actions, and to share the story (or a version of it) in daily conversations with friends, coworkers, and family members. Further, confiding in others enables the storyteller to work on the story, revise it, clarify it, complete it, accept it, and move on (Harvey & Fine, 2006). The construction and actual telling of the story, in fact, are essential elements of the divorce process. Riessman's (1990) analysis of divorce narratives demonstrated that "in their accounts divorcing individuals are active speaking agents who mull over and evaluate their experience in the very process of retelling it" (p. 116).

Importantly, how divorced adults construct their stories influences their adjustment. A divorce narrative may minimize personal culpability in the interest of helping one to feel better about oneself and one's role in the termination of the marriage (Harvey & Fine, 2006). Completing the story allows the individual to experience a sense of closure and catharsis, and sharing the account with others provides opportunities for divorced adults to portray themselves in a socially favorable light. Developing and sharing a story prepares some divorced adults for new relationships, while it assists others in the realization that they do not want to pursue new partners. Research indicates that for individuals who have experienced major losses, there are psychological and physical health benefits for those who open up and disclose emotionally with others about their trauma (Pennebaker, Zech, & Rimé, 2001).

Clearly, there is substantial variation in the development of divorce narratives and in their impact on adjustment. Kellas and Manusov (2003) conducted a fascinating content analysis of 90 breakup narratives and examined associations between characteristics of the narratives and four subdimensions (i.e., emotional disentanglement, grief work, self-worth, and anger) of the Fisher Divorce Adjustment Scale. They found better adjustment among individuals who formed more complete and coherent narratives, those who provided examples, and those who were able to tell their story in a sequential manner. The researchers acknowledged that it was not possible to assess causality in their study, and causation likely flows in both directions, but they observed that adjustment was higher among people who could "impose some sort of logical order and structure to the story—by providing starting and ending points, progressing from one episode to the next, and reflecting the forward progression of events that led to and followed the break-up" (Kellas & Manusov, 2003, p. 301).

In sum, the social construction of divorce narratives appears important for healthy adjustment to divorce, but additional research is necessary to specify the nature of this relationship and to explore the antecedents and consequences of variation in personal accounts. For example, Pennebaker et al. (2001) suggest that some people may not require emotional disclosure to cope effectively. In the next section, we examine gender as a source of variation in postdivorce adjustment.

Similarities and Differences in Men's and Women's Adjustment

The Divorce Variation and Fluidity Model (DVFM) suggests that postdivorce adjustment cannot be understood without considering predivorce individual, marital, and family trajectories. The DVFM also integrates feminist perspectives emphasizing that marital dynamics, parent–child relationships, and other aspects of family life are highly gendered. Applying these insights, an understanding of postdivorce adjustment requires that we consider the gendered nature of marital and family dynamics that predate divorce. Compared with their wives, husbands generally have greater power and exercise the upper hand in marital decision making, they typically spend less time with children and are less directly involved in parenting (Demo & Cox, 2000; Pleck, 1997), and they perform a much smaller share of housework (Bianchi, Robinson, & Milkie, 2006; Erickson, 2005). Women are typically more fully engaged in family life, they assume more psychological responsibility for family activities and family members' needs, they are better attuned to the emotional climate of the marriage, and they are more aware of marital problems (Hetherington, 2003; Hochschild, 2003). As a result, women are more likely than men to have thoughts of divorce (Gager & Sanchez, 2003), they are often less surprised by the divorce and more accepting of the end of their marriage (Arendell, 1995; Emery, 1994; Walzer & Oles, 2003), and they are more likely to initiate divorce (Amato & Irving, 2006; Hetherington & Kelly, 2002). Viewed in this manner, it is understandable that women's and men's contrasting experiences and perceptions of marriage create a context in which their experiences of and adjustment to divorce are also likely to diverge. Given the strongly gendered nature of marital relations in the (often long) period leading up to divorce, the next question is, How do women and men respond similarly and differently to divorce?

Despite numerous studies investigating the influence of gender on postdivorce adjustment, the literature is riddled with inconsistent and contradictory findings. For example, a number of studies found that women and men are equally distressed by divorce (Ross, 1995; Wang & Amato, 2000), and Booth and Amato (1991) found that, controlling for predivorce distress, there was no gender difference in the effect of marital disruption on psychological distress. Similarly, Shapiro (1996) observed that divorced women and remarried women had higher depression levels than their male counterparts, but the difference between divorced women and divorced men was substantially reduced after controlling for economic distress. In a study in Sweden, Gähler (1998) observed lower psychological well-being among divorced men and women compared with their married (and remarried) counterparts, but no significant interaction with gender, indicating that divorce has the same consequences for women and men. Hetherington and Kelly (2002) found that vulnerability to a wide range of illnesses increased among both women and men in the first year following divorce.

Careful reviews of the literature also yield contrasting interpretations of the evidence. A recent review by Braver et al. (2006) concluded that women recover faster following divorce and fare better emotionally than men. Yet Amato's (2000) thorough examination demonstrated that many studies find greater psychological adjustment problems among women following divorce, other studies indicate greater adjustment problems among divorced men, and still other studies find no gender differences, leading the author to conclude that neither gender is more vulnerable emotionally after divorce.

One factor contributing to inconsistent findings and confusion regarding gender differences in the effect of marital dissolution on adult adjustment is that different studies examine different dimensions (and use different measures) of well-being. Accumulating evidence suggests that both women and men are vulnerable in their reactions to divorce and that the difference is in the specific manifestations of stress for women and men. Following divorce, both women and men experience feelings of sadness, loneliness, and depression (Hetherington & Kelly, 2002; Kitson, 1992; Ross, 1995). Divorced women and men also exhibit higher rates of alcohol use than married women and men, respectively (Horwitz et al., 1996; Umberson & Williams, 1993). It appears, however, that women are more likely than men to experience depression following divorce, whereas men are more likely than women to exhibit problematic use of alcohol (Aseltine & Kessler, 1993; Horwitz et al., 1996; Kalmijn & Monden, 2006; Simon & Marcussen, 1999). This pattern holds for both Blacks and Whites, suggesting that women are more likely than men to feel (and to report) symptoms of psychological distress (particularly depression and anxiety) following marital dissolution, whereas separated and divorced men are at greater risk of more severe physical and mental health problems such as substance abuse and dependence (Barrett, 2003; Williams, Takeuchi, & Adair, 1992).

In sum, it appears that much of the confusion surrounding gender differences in adult adjustment to divorce is reconciled by distinguishing among, and identifying the correlates of, specific dimensions of well-being. It is important to understand that, following divorce, both women and men suffer elevated rates of distress that manifest in internalizing and externalizing disorders. In many studies, gender differences are weak in magnitude or statistically nonsignificant after instituting relevant controls. There is a consistent pattern, however, whereby divorced women are vulnerable to depression and divorced men are susceptible to alcohol and other substance problems. Next, we discuss some of the processes that may help to explain why marital dissolution is associated with maladjustment among women and men.

Mechanisms associated with women's and men's postdivorce adjustment. As we have seen, divorce is a major life transition that can wreak havoc on both women and men. Although in many ways women and men experience the same stressful aspects of the divorce process—loss of an intimate relationship, loss of an identity, economic loss, loss of time with children—in other ways there are profound differences in women's and men's experiences of divorce. For example, women typically suffer much harsher economic losses, as we discuss below, and men typically suffer far greater losses in time spent with their children. In short, because the divorce process is gendered, marital dissolution evokes different reactions among women than among men.

Research demonstrates that divorced women are more likely than their married counterparts to experience financial pressure, work stress, and negative life events, which, in turn, are associated with higher levels of depression (Ross, 1995; Simons & Associates, 1996). Further, compared with divorced men, divorced women's greater involvement in family relationships increases their exposure to conflicts and tensions with partners and children from both past marriages and new relationships. These conflicts, combined with women's greater emotional investment in and sensitivity to family relationships, create additional stressors that negatively affect their psychological adjustment. Aside from distress, however, the general psychological profile of divorced women appears more favorable than that of their married counterparts. Marks (1996) examined gender and marital status differences in psychological well-being to test the selection hypothesis that adults with poorer mental health are less successful as marriage partners and thus "select into" divorce. Contrary to the selection argument, Marks found that divorced women had better mental health than married women, rating higher on several relatively enduring personality characteristics, including intelligence, autonomy, and openness to new experience, and scoring lower on neuroticism.

In contrast to divorced women, whose primary burden is the loss of economic support, divorced men suffer most from the loss of social attachment and emotional support (Hetherington & Kelly, 2002; Ross, 1995). For men, marital dissolution means not only the loss of an intimate relationship, but also the accompanying social isolation associated with losing the former wife's emotional labor and her contributions as a kinkeeper who schedules and coordinates activities with nuclear, extended, and chosen kin. Divorced fathers are also less likely than their former spouses to have physical custody of their children, and father–child contact tends to be infrequent and to diminish over time (King et al., 2004). As the divorce process unfolds, many divorced fathers feel they are losing control over their family (Hetherington & Kelly, 2002; Umberson & Williams, 1993). Further, whether there is a basis for their perceptions or not, the vast majority of divorced men feel that the legal system is biased against them, and they are much less likely than their former spouses to be satisfied with the provisions of their divorce agreements (Braver et al., 2006).

It is perhaps not surprising then that many recently divorced men are vulnerable to potentially serious emotional and behavioral disorders. Marks (1996) found that, unlike the generally positive profiles she observed for midlife divorced women, separated or divorced men rated more poorly than their married counterparts on a wide array of psychological measures. Specifically, they scored significantly lower on desirable characteristics such as intelligence, extraversion, conscientiousness, self-acceptance, environmental mastery, positive relations with others, and purpose in life, and they rated higher on undesirable characteristics such as neuroticism and hostility-irritability. In support of the view that distress among divorced men is primarily attributable to the loss of emotional support, research suggests that a new intimate relationship appears to erase many of these differences in psychological adjustment (Hetherington & Kelly, 2002). This pattern of findings can also be interpreted as support for feminist views that male privilege benefits men in marriages and that they suffer in many ways when they lose this set of privileges.

Variation in Socioemotional Adjustment Within and Across Racial Groups

Although limited research has focused on race as a source of variation in adjustment to marital dissolution, the available evidence suggests that divorce is similarly distressing across racial and ethnic groups (Amato, 2000), and there is substantial within-race variation in how adults respond to divorce (Lawson & Thompson, 1999). A number of studies reported no differences in mean adjustment levels between divorced Whites and Blacks (Aldous & Ganey, 1999; Wang & Amato, 2000), or among Whites, Blacks, and Mexican Americans (Neff & Schluter, 1993). However, other studies have suggested that Blacks have less difficulty than Whites in adjusting to divorce (Kitson, 1992; Williams et al., 1992), due at least in part to more tolerant norms and less stigma regarding divorce in African American communities (Orbuch & Brown, 2006).

Williams et al. (1992) observed that among both Blacks and Whites, divorced men and women had higher rates of psychiatric disorders than their married peers. Separated or divorced Black men exhibited alcohol abuse at a rate 4 times that of their married counterparts; similarly, alcohol abuse among divorced White men was 3.6 times higher than among married White men. In comparison with their married counterparts, separated and divorced Black women reported elevated rates of alcohol and drug use, and separated-divorced White women exhibited higher rates of all psychiatric disorders examined. In terms of the magnitude of the effect of marital dissolution on psychiatric disorder, the association was stronger for White men than for Black men and was much stronger for White women than for Black women.

Other research suggests that the nature and timing of marital dissolution are important considerations in understanding how individuals in different racial and ethnic groups respond to marital transitions. Separation is a more common experience among Blacks than among Whites, and separation tends to be a more protracted experience for Blacks (Broman, 2002), often including periods of reconciliation (Weinberg & McCarthy, 1993). Barrett (2003) found that adjustment to the separation experience was more problematic and stressful for Whites, but divorce was associated with greater maladjustment among Blacks. Specifically, separated Whites were significantly more depressed than separated Blacks, but among the divorced, Blacks exhibited higher rates of substance use and dependence than their White counterparts. These findings corroborate the view expressed throughout the book that marital dissolution is a multifaceted process and that the occurrence and timing of legal divorce are not good markers of the beginning of the process.

In sum, it appears there is greater variation in the consequences of marital dissolution within racial and ethnic groups than across groups, but much more work is needed to understand the sources, magnitude, and duration of the variation.

Personal Growth and Maturation Following Divorce

The prevailing paradigm in divorce research (see Chapter 3) involves carefully documenting the harmful consequences of marital disruption for family members, and corroborating evidence for such outcomes is abundant, as reviewed in this chapter and elsewhere. Although there can be no question that divorce is a stressful experience, accumulating evidence indicates that marital dissolution also evokes positive outcomes. Research suggests that divorced women and men exhibit more autonomy, self-confidence, and personal growth than their married peers (Acock & Demo, 1994; Marks, 1996; Tashiro & Frazier, 2003). Kitson (1992) observed a uniform pattern among Blacks and Whites and among women and men, whereby newly divorced adults were substantially more likely than their married peers to report personal growth, which is not surprising given that they described their former marriages as unfulfilling, constraining, and alienating.

Others have noted that major life transitions can have beneficial consequences for mental health, particularly when the transition involves exiting a marriage that was highly stressful and conflictual (Amato & Hohmann-Marriott, 2007; Ross, 1995) or when there was a history of major depression prior to divorce (Cohen, Klein, & O'Leary, 2007). Aseltine and Kessler (1993) documented significant variation in adjustment according to divorced adults' perceptions of their recently dissolved marriages. They observed higher depression among respondents who reported no serious marital problems at the baseline assessment and significantly lower depression among those who reported such problems. Similarly, Booth and Amato (1991) found that increased depression 2 years postdivorce was associated with reports of few marital troubles.

This pattern of findings suggests that divorce may be a relief for those who endured troubled marriages (Johnson & Wu, 2002; Wheaton, 1990), while it can be shocking and disturbing to those who judged their marriages favorably.

Commonly reported reactions to divorce include relief, freedom, and independence (Colburn, Lin, & Moore, 1992; Stewart et al., 1997; Tashiro & Frazier, 2003). Hetherington's (Hetherington & Kelly, 2002) longitudinal research found that three fourths of her sample of divorced women were happier 2 years postdivorce than they were prior to separation, and an analysis of the National Survey of Families and Households found that, following divorce, single mothers were more satisfied with their parenting roles and social lives than they were during their marriage (Acock & Demo, 1994).

A balanced and accurate portrait of divorce entails recognition that positive outcomes such as growth and autonomy coexist with negative outcomes such as depression and substance use (Tashiro, Frazier, & Berman, 2006). For example, Hetherington and Kelly (2002) observed that many newly divorced individuals immersed themselves in self-improvement programs, changed jobs, entered therapy, and enhanced their physical appearance. Qualitative studies demonstrate that divorce provides myriad opportunities to learn new ways of "doing gender" (Walzer, 2008) and that recently divorced women and men employ elaborate strategies to correct personal shortcomings, develop new competencies and identities, explore new leisure activities, and become more proficient in negotiating daily life as single heads of households (Riessman, 1990).

As with other dimensions of adjustment we have examined, there is considerable variation in personal growth following divorce. Hetherington and Kelly (2002) found that nearly one third of the women and men they studied could be described as "winners" 10 years after divorce. One group, comprising 20% of their sample, was characterized as *enhancers*, divorced adults who were autonomous and self-confident, who displayed remarkable growth in the decade following their divorce, and who typically repartnered. A second and smaller group, consisting of 10% of their sample, was classified as *competent loners*. The latter group was well adjusted and led active and fulfilling lives, but differed from the former group in that they felt complete without pursuing a new partner. In sum, it is common for divorce to provide opportunities for self-improvement, growth, and development, and at least a sizable minority of divorced adults embrace themselves in such change (Stewart et al., 1997). In the next section, we describe fluidity in adjustment throughout the divorce process and explore factors associated with variability in adult adjustment over time.

Variation in Adult Socioemotional Adjustment Over Time

An important and frequently overlooked consideration in explaining adjustment difficulties among divorced individuals is that, as suggested by the DVFM (Figure 2.1), their maladjustment often precedes divorce. Several longitudinal studies have found that prior to marital dissolution, the average level of well-being of married men and women who later divorce is significantly lower than that of their peers who remain married (Booth & Amato, 1991; Kim & McKenry, 2002; Mastekaasa, 1994). Further, in the period leading up to the divorce, psychological well-being appears to decline and reports of distress seem to increase. Booth and Amato provide evidence that unhappiness and psychological distress increase as much as 3 years prior to divorce, while more severe psychophysiological symptoms (headaches, cold sweats, acid stomach) increase in the final year preceding divorce, suggesting that there are accumulating and heightening stresses as the divorce approaches.

Studies examining the first two waves of the National Survey of Families and Households demonstrate that individuals who were married at Wave 1 and divorced by Wave 2 reported significantly more depressive symptoms prior to marital dissolution than did their counterparts who remained married (Kim & McKenry, 2002; Simon & Marcussen, 1999). Research involving other samples also indicates that, compared with wives who remained married, those who later divorced exhibited significantly poorer psychological adjustment over a period of several years prior to their divorce. Mastekaasa (1994, 1997) documented diminished psychological well-being and elevated alcohol use as early as 4 years prior to divorce; Horwitz et al. (1996) observed greater depression among wives as much as 7 years prior to divorce; and Davies et al. (1997) found developmental trajectories of depression for many divorced women that could be traced to adversities during childhood. This pattern of findings is important because it suggests that a) divorce is not necessarily a cause of personal adjustment problems that are observed in the period following marital dissolution, and b) even when divorce is a cause of exacerbated adjustment problems after divorce, it is only one among an array of likely causal factors.

With consistent evidence that social and emotional maladjustment predates divorce, how long do personal difficulties persist following marital dissolution? Analyses of national longitudinal data indicated that those who divorced experienced a significant increase in depression from preseparation (T1) to postseparation (T2), a period covering 5 years (Kim & McKenry, 2002; Simon & Marcussen, 1999). In another study, Booth and Amato (1991) examined three waves of panel data and found that all three of their measures of psychological stress (unhappiness, psychological distress, and psychosomatic symptoms) were elevated for 2 years following divorce and then returned to the participants' baseline levels or within the "normal" range on the measures, even among those who were most disadvantaged. Lorenz et al. (1997) reported that depression increased markedly after divorce and then decreased over the next 3 years. Kitson (1992) observed significant improvement in levels of subjective distress, physical illnesses, and self-esteem from the time of filing for divorce to a second measurement 1 year postdivorce. In her study, differences between the divorced and those who remained married declined substantially after the first year, and by 4 years postdivorce, psychological functioning was comparable to that of individuals who remained married. Collectively, these findings indicate substantial temporal change or fluidity in adjustment. More longitudinal studies are necessary to better understand the duration of disruptions in well-being, but it appears that, on average, adjustment problems persist for 2 to 3 years following divorce, with symptoms diminishing in frequency and severity after the first year. These findings also support the view that divorce is a crisis that passes with time, rather than a chronic stressor.

An alternative view, however, is that while divorce represents a crisis that creates temporary or short-term disturbances for some individuals, for others divorce is a chronic strain that causes permanent adjustment problems (Amato, 2000). This view recognizes both fluidity and individual variation in adjustment trajectories following divorce. For example, Kitson (1992) found that during the first 2 years postdivorce, 73% of her sample reported no or minimal depression, 13% exhibited mild to moderate depression, and 14% suffered moderate to severe depression. Hetherington and Kelly (2002) observed that 10 years after divorce, 10% of their study participants (whom they termed the *defeated*) were still suffering from depression, despair, and despondency. A more favorable profile appears to characterize the majority of adults, for whom the common experience is a combination of persisting pain and personal growth following divorce. The largest group in Hetherington and Kelly's study (termed the *good enoughs*) exhibited persistent vulnerabilities, but they also displayed strengths and competencies that helped them to construct better lives following divorce than they had before divorce.

≋ FINANCIAL ADJUSTMENT

For most divorcing women and men, divorce means a series of financial adjustments and setbacks. For some, the losses will be relatively minor, whereas for others, divorce means prolonged economic hardship. There is consistent evidence that divorced women suffer worse economic consequences than divorced men, including lower family incomes and higher poverty rates (Casper & Bianchi, 2002). In an authoritative review of recent research on the financial costs of divorce, Sayer (2006) reports that estimates of the average loss in family income that women experience over the period from preseparation to one year postseparation range from 27% to 51%; for men, the corresponding estimates range from losses of 8% to 41%. Often overlooked, however, is that there is substantial within-gender variation (Braver et al., 2006). Some divorced women and men fare quite well following divorce, while others endure prolonged periods of economic stress and deprivation.

A variety of factors contribute to the harsh economic consequences that women typically encounter following divorce. Women's greater involvement in parenting and other family activities both prior to and following divorce restricts their educational and occupational opportunities, and these problems are compounded by the gender gap in earnings. Women are more likely than men to work in low-paying, temporary, and part-time jobs, and women's childbearing and childrearing activities cause interruptions in their employment histories. Further, although most dependent-aged children live with their mothers following divorce, thereby increasing mothers' expenses, and although compliance with child support orders has improved with recent legislation, many divorced mothers receive irregular or partial child support payments from their former husbands, and 25% receive no child support (Casper & Bianchi, 2002; Manning & Smock, 2000). Sadly, most divorced women and their children do not recover financially for at least 5 years following dissolution, unless mothers remarry (Hetherington & Kelly, 2002).

Economic adjustment to divorce is highly variable, however, and research has identified a number of protective factors that are associated with higher postdivorce family income. Divorced women who are better off financially are those who were employed more hours per week prior to dissolution, had higher predivorce incomes, received more education, and had continuous employment histories (Smock, Manning, & Gupta, 1999). As many as one fifth of divorced women experience an improvement in their standard of living following dissolution, and approximately 1 in 10 fare better economically than their former husbands (Bianchi, Subaiya, & Kahn, 1999). On the other hand, the majority of divorced women endure harsh economic realities associated with marital dissolution, and one third of divorced women are forced to relinquish ownership of their home (Hanson, McLanahan, & Thomson, 1998).

Although not as commonly recognized, a number of factors combine to cause economic stress and setbacks for men following marital dissolution. Analyzing longitudinal data from the Panel Study of Income Dynamics, McManus and DiPrete (2001) documented that two important sources of economic decline for divorced men are an inability to compensate for their former partners' income and an increase in both mandatory and voluntary support payments to their former wives and children. The researchers found that following divorce, White men lose approximately one third of their total household income and experience a decline in living standards of 11% to 20%. McManus and DiPrete also observed substantial heterogeneity in men's economic adjustment to divorce, demonstrating that although there is a sizable minority of men who can be classified as economic "winners" following divorce, the clear majority are modest to moderate economic "losers." Further, Braver et al. (2006) argue that because previous research has neglected a) tax consequences for divorcing parents and b) nonresidential fathers' voluntary support payments (e.g., visitation expenses), divorced fathers' economic losses, after-tax income, and standard of living are worse than is generally assumed. Many divorced fathers do not have adequate income even to support themselves, thus restricting their ability to support former wives and children (Nelson, 2004).

A smaller body of work illustrates variation in economic adjustment across and within racial and ethnic groups. In the aggregate, because they have less savings to fall back on and lower incomes, Black women and men experience somewhat sharper declines in family income following marital disruption (measured in percentages) than their White counterparts (McManus & DiPrete, 2001; Smock, 1993). A small group of African

American men, those contributing 80% or more to predisruption family income, may see little or no change in their postdisruption standard of living, but the more common scenario is a 13% to 20% decline in standard of living (McManus & DiPrete, 2001). Among Hispanics, Stroup and Pollock (1999) found that divorced men had comparable incomes to married men, but divorced women's incomes declined 24%. In sum, the limited evidence on economic adjustment among Blacks and Hispanics is quite consistent with widely replicated patterns observed among White women and men.

☰ RELATIONS BETWEEN FORMER SPOUSES AND COPARENTING

In the aftermath of dissolving a marriage and confronting the social, emotional, legal, and economic challenges accompanying the divorce process, another challenge facing many divorced adults is to negotiate a new relationship as former spouses and coparents. Whether they actively pursue it or grudgingly tolerate it, most individuals maintain at least some contact with their former partners, continue to care about them, and provide support for each other in times of need or crisis (Hetherington & Kelly, 2002; Kitson, 1992; Masuda, 2006). Perhaps ex-spouses' greatest challenge is to construct new parenting arrangements that cross two or more households.

Several studies have described considerable variation in the nature of relationships forged between former spouses. Kitson (1992) asked divorced adults to characterize how they felt about their ex-spouses at 2 years postseparation. She found that one fourth reported that they "still liked" their former partner, one fourth said they "don't feel much of anything" toward them, nearly one fourth felt sorry for them, and smaller proportions expressed love, hatred, or both love and hatred toward them. Participants in Kitson's study reported moderate and even strong feelings of anger toward their former spouses during the first year following separation, but angry feelings subsided markedly during the second year. Contact between former spouses 1 year following divorce varied widely. For example, more than half had talked with their former spouse by telephone, and more than one third had talked in person over the previous few weeks, but more than one third had no contact at all.

An important component of healthy adjustment to divorce is a successful transition to coparenting, or sharing of parenting responsibilities across households (Amato, 2000; Baum, 2003). Research on coparenting reveals that divorced adults adopt a variety of strategies to carry out their childrearing activities. Ahrons's research, which followed families who had experienced divorce over 2 decades, suggested a typology consisting of five different coparenting styles: *perfect pals* (who maintain friendly relationships and talk with each other every week), *cooperative colleagues* (who collaborate as parents but otherwise do not have relationships with each other), *angry associates* (who maintain regular contact but frequently disagree and argue with each other), *fiery foes* (who avoid contact but are angry whenever they interact), and *dissolved duos* (who no longer have a relationship with each other).

Other influential studies have yielded similar typologies and, in doing so, have further substantiated the extensive variability in postdivorce parenting arrangements. Maccoby and Mnookin's (1992) analysis of a large sample of divorced families identified four types of coparenting relationships: *conflicted* (low cooperation and high discord, comprising 34% of their sample at 18 months postseparation), *disengaged* (low communication and low discord, 29%), *cooperative* (high cooperation and low discord, 26%), and *mixed* (high cooperation and high discord, 11%). As time since the divorce passed, Maccoby and Mnookin found that the incidence of conflicted coparenting declined and disengagement increased so that by 3.5 years postdivorce, the mixed group was the modal coparenting arrangement. Hetherington and Kelly's (2002) longitudinal research largely corroborates these findings. They found that 6 years after divorce, the largest group of divorced parents (half of their sample) was engaged in parallel parenting, essentially ignoring each other and thus avoiding conflict. Roughly one fourth of Hetherington and Kelly's divorced parents were characterized by conflicted parenting and one fourth by cooperative parenting.

In sum, most divorced individuals maintain at least some contact with their former spouses. Although conflict, hostility, and antagonism often characterize these relationships in the immediate aftermath of divorce, these negative dynamics generally diminish over time as anger subsides, new lives are formed, and interaction between former spouses becomes less frequent. As these changes are occurring, similar processes are transforming coparenting relationships: Conflict declines and disengagement increases with time since divorce. It bears reiterating, however, that although these changes describe the modal pattern, there is substantial variation, including lingering hostilities, both overt and covert, with children often caught in the middle.

CONCLUSIONS

Although most divorced adults endure a period of social, emotional, and financial difficulties following the termination of their marriage, there is substantial variation in the nature, magnitude, and duration of problems they encounter. The research evidence also suggests change over time, or fluidity, in adult adjustment to divorce. For many divorced adults, social and emotional difficulties predate divorce and remain elevated for 2 to 3 years following divorce. A small minority of divorced adults suffer chronic strain that lingers for many years. Although less commonly recognized, divorce is also associated with feelings of personal growth and maturation. A broader, more dynamic and nuanced perspective on family transitions associated with divorce captures not only the stress, turmoil, and disturbances in well-being that characterize the process of marital dissolution, but also the accompanying positive life changes and feelings of autonomy, personal growth, and maturation. Two processes that contribute to upward trajectories in adult well-being that surface 2 to 3 years postdivorce are improving financial situations and more harmonious coparenting dynamics. In the next chapter, we explore factors associated with variation in children's adjustment to divorce.

8

Variation and Fluidity in Children's Adjustment to Divorce

U nlike the majority of adults who divorce more or less voluntarily, parental divorce is imposed upon children. Some children, particularly older ones, may have seen it coming, whereas others are completely unprepared and do not know what to expect or how to act. Initial reactions include feelings of shock, anger, confusion, disappointment, and even distress. How long do these feelings last and how common is it for children to suffer more serious adjustment problems, such as blaming and doubting themselves (e.g., low self-esteem), becoming depressed or anxious, performing poorly in school, or acting out (e.g., lying, cheating, stealing, alcohol and drug use)? How much variation is there in children's adjustment to divorce, and what factors are associated with that variation? How do children's reactions change as time unfolds?

In this chapter, we explore variation and fluidity in children's adjustment to their parents' divorce. First, we examine several outcomes on which children and adolescents in divorcing families commonly perform worse than their peers in nondisrupted families, including academic achievement, externalizing behaviors, and intimate relationships. We then review evidence on psychological adjustment among young adults whose parents have divorced, including a discussion of the increased risk of their marriages ending in divorce. Next, we discuss variation in postdivorce family processes, including mechanisms that may be linked to child and adolescent adjustment. In the concluding section, we examine fluidity in children's adjustment over time, including areas of personal growth and maturation.

DIMENSIONS OF CHILD ADJUSTMENT

There is abundant evidence that, in the aggregate, children who have experienced parental divorce fare worse on several indicators of social, emotional, academic, and behavioral adjustment than their counterparts in families with continuously married parents. Methodologically rigorous studies (Amato & Afifi, 2006; Aseltine, 1996; Buchanan, Maccoby, & Dornbusch, 1996; Capaldi & Patterson, 1991; Demo & Acock, 1996a; Furstenberg & Teitler, 1994; Hetherington & Kelly, 2002; McLanahan & Sandefur, 1994; Morrison & Cherlin, 1995; Simons & Associates, 1996; Sun & Li, 2002) as well as authoritative reviews and meta-analyses (Amato, 2001; Barber & Demo, 2006; Kunz, 2001; Reifman, Villa, Amans, Rethinam, & Telesca, 2001) consistently indicate adverse effects of parental divorce on child, adolescent, and young adult adjustment. However, researchers' understanding of the divorce process and its consequences has been restricted because some important issues have received far less research attention, notably including the duration of and variation in effects. In this chapter, we acknowledge the modal pattern whereby child adjustment is disturbed following parental divorce, and we concentrate on the nature, extent, and correlates of variability in adjustment both in the short term and in the long term. In each section below, we briefly review the literature on differences between children in divorced and first-marriage families and then focus on the issues of variability and fluidity in children's reactions and adjustment.

Children's Initial Reactions

Variability in children's reactions to parental divorce is evident as soon as they are notified of the news. Based on interviews with parents of children ages 6 to 12, Stewart et al. (1997) found that approximately half of the children responded to news of the separation with distress or sadness, fewer than 1 in 10 (9%) were angry, a similar proportion (8%) were relieved, and the remainder either asked questions or had no visible reactions. When children themselves were asked to describe their feelings upon hearing that their parents were separating, they described a wide range of emotional responses. Reflecting a sense of loss, the most common reaction (reported by half of the children) was sadness. Other emotions children reported feeling "a lot" included being confused (22%), scared (22%), surprised (15%), angry (13%), and glad (11%).

By 1-year postseparation, children were feeling better and stronger, feelings of sadness and guilt had receded, but a small percentage (9%) continued to feel angry. In sum, although the prevailing initial reactions were negative in tone, a substantial minority of children eventually described themselves as being relieved or glad. For many children, parental divorce signals a transition in family relationships whereby daily tensions, bickering, and hostility between parents subside, creating hope for a happier family environment.

Academic Achievement

On average, children of divorce do more poorly than their peers on various measures of academic performance, including grade point averages, standardized test scores, and educational attainment. For example, children whose parents divorced are more likely to drop out of high school than their peers with continuously married parents (Furstenberg & Teitler, 1994; McLanahan & Sandefur, 1994; Pong & Ju, 2000). Research shows that differences across family types tend to be small, however, and these differences often are no longer significant when other relevant variables are taken into consideration. For example, studies have documented that many children who are not doing well academically following divorce were not doing well prior to marital dissolution (Morrison & Cherlin, 1995; Sun & Li, 2001), which suggests that their poorer performance may have been due to factors other than the divorce itself. Other studies have found that deficits in academic performance and educational attainment among adolescents whose parents divorced were substantially reduced in magnitude after taking changes in socioeconomic status into account, which suggests that the lower academic performance is as much due to lower levels of socioeconomic resources as the divorce itself (Emery, 1999; McLanahan & Sandefur, 1994; Pong & Ju, 2000; Sun & Li, 2002, 2007).

With reference to variability, Morrison and Cherlin's (1995) analysis of the National Longitudinal Study of Youth illustrated significant variation in children's achievement on reading tests following parental divorce. For example, nearly three in five boys (59%) and nearly half of girls (47%) from divorced families scored within the average range (within half a standard deviation above or below the mean) on a reading comprehension test 1 year after marital disruption. At the same time, roughly one fourth of boys (23%) and girls (24%) whose parents divorced scored below average, while a significant minority (19% of boys and 29% of girls) scored more than a half standard deviation above average. Kurdek, Fine, and Sinclair (1995) showed that there is within-divorced-group variability (see Chapter 3) in a number of adjustment dimensions, including school achievement and conduct problems. These researchers assessed whether there were differences in children's school achievement depending on how many times they had experienced parental divorce. Children who experienced multiple divorces had significantly lower grades than those who had experienced divorce only once.

With respect to fluidity, Morrison and Cherlin (1995) compared children's rankings on reading achievement at a baseline measurement prior to family disruption and then at a follow-up 1 year postdisruption. They found that there was no change for half the sample (50% of boys and 57% of girls), whereas scores declined for roughly one in three boys (29%) and girls (32%), and reading comprehension improved for a smaller group of children (21% of boys and 11% of girls).

Internalizing Behaviors

In the aftermath of parental divorce, children and adolescents experience lower average (mean) levels of psychological adjustment and self-esteem and higher levels of depression and anxiety than their peers in nondisrupted two-parent families (Amato, 2001; Barber & Demo, 2006). The differences between groups are typically modest (Aseltine, 1996) or weak (Amato, 2001), however, and often disappear when relevant variables such as socioeconomic status, predivorce family characteristics, and children's prior adjustment are controlled (Aseltine, 1996; Demo & Acock, 1996a; Strohschein, 2005; Videon, 2002).

One way to appreciate the extent of variation characterizing children's psychological adjustment following divorce is to recognize that tests of statistical significance for differences between children in various family types often yield nonsignificant results (e.g., Demo & Acock, 1996a; Videon, 2002). This indicates that differences in self-esteem, depression, anxiety, or other indicators of children's adjustment are greater within family types than across family types. For example, examining data from the National Longitudinal Study of Adolescent Health, Videon (2002) found that for both boys and girls, there were no differences in depression between adolescents who experienced parental separation or divorce and those living in nondisrupted families. In contrast, Halpern-Meekin and Tach (2008) reported that both stepchildren and shared children in blended families reported more depressive symptoms than adolescents in first-marriage families.

Several studies have indicated that there is within-divorce-group variation in adolescent depression. Videon (2002), despite finding no significant differences among family types, found substantial differences within family types. In families in which parents divorced, adolescents who reported positive and satisfying relationships with their opposite-sex parent experienced significantly fewer depressive symptoms than their peers with less satisfying parent–adolescent relationships. Using both parent and adolescent reports, Oldehinkel et al. (2008) found that girls in postdivorce families were more vulnerable than boys to depression during adolescence and experienced greater depression in middle adolescence than during early adolescence. Aseltine (1996) observed that adolescents were more likely to be depressed following parental divorce if they suffered economic hardship and were less likely to be depressed if their parents later remarried.

Evidence from longitudinal studies illustrates the fluid nature of children's and adolescents' psychological adjustment to parental divorce. During the period when parents are separating and for the first 2 years following divorce, family tensions tend to be salient and stressful, and children's well-being declines. Strohschein (2005) tracked a nationally representative sample of children who were ages 4 to 7 and living with their two biological parents at baseline. She found that that even before parental divorce, children whose parents would later divorce experienced higher levels of anxiety and depression and that upon divorce and its accompanying life changes, child anxiety-depression increased by 28%. Videon (2002) found that for both boys and girls, postdivorce depressive symptoms were predicted by predivorce depression. Many studies find, however, that over time children adapt to their new living arrangements, and their psychological well-being improves (Ahrons, 2004; Harvey & Fine, 2004; Hetherington & Kelly, 2002; Jekielek, 1998). Aseltine (1996) suggests that parental divorce may facilitate children's ability to elicit social support from parents, peers, and others, strengthening their resistance to later family turmoil.

Externalizing Behaviors

A widely studied topic in divorce research is the consequences of marital dissolution for children's conduct problems or externalizing behaviors.

One reason this research question receives so much scholarly attention is that conduct problems appear to be the aspect of children's functioning most seriously influenced by divorce. Rigorous meta-analyses conducted by Amato (2001; Amato & Keith, 1991) indicated stronger effect sizes (i.e., a measure of the magnitude of differences between groups) for conduct problems (approximately one fourth of a standard deviation) than for other dimensions of children's behavior such as psychological adjustment, self-concept, and social adjustment (for which effect sizes averaged one tenth of a standard deviation).

Studies consistently report that, on average, children whose parents have divorced experience more behavioral problems (e.g., aggression, disruptive behavior), engage in more delinquent activities, and exhibit higher rates of alcohol and drug use than their peers living with continuously married parents (Carlson, 2006; Emery, Waldron, Kitzmann, & Aaron, 1999; Lee, 2002; Pett, Wampold, Turner, & Vaughan-Cole, 1999; Strohschein, 2005; Videon, 2002). Simons and Associates (1996) found that delinquency was higher among both boys and girls from divorced families than among their peers with parents in either happy or distressed first marriages. Specifically, boys and girls with divorced parents were more likely to shoplift, purposely damage property, run away from home, be drunk in a public place, be picked up by the police, or have gone to court. In addition, Hoffmann's (2002) examination of National Educational Longitudinal Study data found that, across a variety of community contexts, drug use was significantly higher among adolescents living in single-mother, single-father, and step-parent households than among their peers living in households headed by two biological parents.

Whereas these results suggest that family structure effects are robust, there is also evidence from within-divorce-group studies indicating that proximal family processes (such as parenting behaviors) associated with divorce also exert important influences on adolescent behavior. For example, behavior problems among children who have experienced parental divorce are directly associated with parents' use of negative control (i.e., disapproval, criticism, and hostile threats) (Pett et al., 1999). Further, the behaviors of both residential and nonresidential parents are important. Research has observed fewer conduct problems among adolescents from divorced families with a highly involved nonresidential father compared with those with a relatively uninvolved nonresidential father (Carlson, 2006).

Notwithstanding the importance of the consistent finding that children whose parents have divorced are more likely to engage in externalizing and antisocial behaviors, there is sizable variation in this aspect of children's functioning. Morrison and Cherlin (1995) tracked changes in children's behavior problems during the year immediately following the disruption of their parents' marriage and found that, in the aggregate, parental divorce was associated with no significant changes in girls' behavior and modest negative changes in boys' behavior. Beyond mean differences, however, Morrison and Cherlin observed substantial variation. For example, following disruption, nearly half of boys (49%) and girls (43%) scored within the average range (within half of a standard deviation above or below the mean) on the Behavior Problems Index. However, a large minority of boys (42%) and nearly one third of girls (31%) exhibited more problems than average (more than half a standard deviation above the mean).

Similarly, Hoffmann's (2002) analysis documented considerable variation in drug use among adolescents living in different family types, with higher use among boys, Whites, adolescents who moved more often, those who dropped out of school, and those reporting lower levels of attachment to parents. His findings also showed variation in drug use by children's postdivorce living arrangements. He estimated that compared with drug use among adolescents living with both biological parents, drug use was approximately 13% higher in mother-only and mother-stepfather households, 23% higher in father-only households, and 25% higher in father-stepmother households. In sum, there is accumulating evidence of substantial variation in children's adjustment to divorce and of the importance of children's living arrangements and relationships with parents in accounting for this variation.

In terms of fluidity, nearly half (48%) of boys and girls exhibited no change on the Behavior Problems Index over the 2-year period spanning pre-disruption to 1 year postdisruption. Over the same period, scores worsened for one third of the sample (35% of boys and 33% of girls), and scores improved for nearly one in five boys (18%) and girls (19%). Thus, similar to the pattern reported earlier for children's academic achievement, the occurrence of behavior problems did not change for nearly half of the children in the year following divorce, but such problems increased in frequency for more than one third of children and decreased for a smaller proportion.

Intimate Relationships and Adolescent Sexual Behavior

Research consistently supports an association between parental divorce and both early debut of sexual activity (Ellis et al., 2003; Furstenberg &

Teitler, 1994; Simons & Associates, 1996; Upchurch, Aneshensel, Sucoff, & Levy-Storms, 1999) and the probability of adolescent childbearing (Ellis et al., 2003; Furstenberg & Teitler, 1994; McLanahan & Sandefur, 1994). Upchurch et al. (1999) reported earlier onset and higher rates of sexual activity among boys and girls in single-parent families and stepfamilies than among their peers with two biological parents. For example, boys' median age at sexual initiation was 17.3 years in families with two biological parents, compared with 16 in single-parent families and 15 in stepfamilies.

The behaviors and attitudes of residential parents (typically mothers) and nonresidential parents (typically fathers) largely account for the increased likelihood of early sex among children of divorce. For example, compared with parents in other family types, divorced parents are more likely to have permissive sexual attitudes and are less likely to closely monitor their children's activities. Divorced parents' greater acceptance of adolescent sexual activity, their greater tendency to engage in (and thus model) nonmarital sexual relationships, and their more sporadic supervision of their teenage children adversely affect children's romantic relationships and increase the risk of teen sexual activity (Bartell, 2006; Simons & Associates, 1996). For example, divorced parents are less likely to discourage their children's relationships with peers who may be sexually active.

A final illustration of the effects of divorce on interpersonal relationships is referred to as the *intergenerational transmission of divorce*. Even though research suggests that divorce has relatively modest effects on young adults' romantic relationships, adults whose parents have divorced have a slightly, but significantly, higher likelihood of divorce than do adults whose parents never divorced. The reasons for this intergenerational effect are not entirely clear, but could be due to young adults of divorce being more willing to end unhappy relationships because they have witnessed their parents do so, possessing more favorable attitudes toward divorce, inheriting certain undesirable personality characteristics from their parents (e.g., neuroticism, narcissism, depression-proneness), and observing and learning unhealthy relationship interactions (Amato & DeBoer, 2001; Bartell, 2006; Wolfinger, 2005). Most likely, the intergenerational transmission of divorce effect is caused by some combination of genetically based personality dispositions and modeling effects.

With respect to variation among individuals who have experienced parental divorce, Jacquet and Surra (2001) interviewed men and women ages 19 to 35 and found that parental divorce exerts modest effects on young women's heterosexual relationships. Compared with their peers whose parents were continuously married, young women with divorced parents reported less trust in their partners, less relationship satisfaction, more love for their partners, and more ambivalence, conflict, and negativity. Parental divorce appeared to influence young men differently, with effects contingent on whether their partners' parents were also divorced. For example, in marriages in which both partners experienced parental divorce, men reported less trust in their partners' honesty and benevolence. But in comparison to men in marriages in which both parties experienced parental divorce, men in marriages in which just the man had experienced parental divorce reported greater trust in their partners' benevolence. These findings are consistent with a large body of research and theory suggesting that, compared with men, women are socialized to value intimate relationships to a greater extent and invest more heavily in them (Hays, 1996; Hochschild, 2003). When parental divorce occurs, women may respond with more caution in their own relationships.

Interestingly, Jacquet and Surra (2001) observed that reports of friendship-based love among young women whose parents divorced were characterized by significantly greater variation than those of their counterparts in nondisrupted families. Reflecting on the wide variation in children's experiences and responses leading up to and following marital dissolution, Jacquet and Surra concluded that "parental divorce may induce a fear of intimacy and mistrust, or it may invoke a more realistic understanding of relationships. Young adults whose parents divorce probably take multiple pathways as they negotiate the terrain of heterosexual relationships" (p. 637). Unfortunately, researchers know little about variability and fluidity in children's intimate relationships and sexual behavior following divorce because few methodologically rigorous studies have followed families through the divorce process to examine changes in these behaviors.

〰 VARIABILITY IN POSTDIVORCE FAMILY PROCESSES

Recognizing that family processes following divorce are likely to vary substantially from one family to another, researchers have examined family processes that are theoretically relevant for understanding children's postdivorce adjustment. In studies that Barber and Demo (2006) classify as Tier 2 research, investigators have conceptualized proximal family processes as mediators of the impact of divorce on child and adolescent adjustment. Two family processes that have been strongly supported as mediators of this relationship are interparental conflict and the quality and nature of nonresidential parenting.

As is the case for conflict between parents prior to divorce, the amount and nature of interparental conflict following divorce are highly variable. Maccoby and Mnookin (1992) reported that in the second year postseparation, one fourth of divorced couples were cooperative in their coparenting, one third were conflicted, nearly one third were disengaged, and the remainder could be characterized as mixed in that they vascillated between cooperation and conflict. Ahrons (2004) characterized 40% of the couples in her study as cooperative during the first few years postdivorce and 60% as still angry and highly conflictual. Hetherington and Kelly's (2002) analysis indicated that 20% to 25% of couples remained highly conflicted at an assessment 6 years following divorce, while roughly one fourth of couples were cooperative with one another, and the largest group, comprising half her sample, were engaged in parallel parenting, essentially ignoring each other.

Nonresidential parenting following divorce is typically performed by single or remarried fathers, and research documents substantial variation in paternal contact and other dimensions of divorced fathers' relationships with their children. For example, estimates based on two nationally representative surveys indicate that more than one fifth of children living apart from their fathers did not see their fathers at all in the previous year, and one fourth saw their fathers less than once per month (King, 1994; Stewart, 1999). Yet the same studies document that more than one fourth of children with nonresident fathers saw their fathers at least weekly, and nearly one third spent extended periods of time with their fathers. A follow-up examining a third national sample revealed variation by race-ethnicity and education in many aspects of nonresident father involvement, with highest levels of involvement among highly educated, White fathers and lowest levels among White fathers with a high school education or less (King et al., 2004). Among the smaller group of children with nonresident mothers, Stewart (1999) found somewhat higher levels of parent–child contact than she observed among children with nonresident fathers. She documented substantial variation, however, with 15% of nonresident mothers not seeing their children at all in the previous year and 10% seeing them only once during the year, whereas 42% saw their children at least once per week.

⁂ VARIATIONS IN CHILDREN'S RESPONSES TO DIVORCE

Variations in children's responses to divorce do not occur randomly or without any systematic patterns across subgroups. Below, we review evidence concerning two key variables that have been examined as possible moderators of children's reactions to parental divorce: children's gender and age.

Variations by children's gender. There are conceptual reasons to suspect that children's gender may be a moderator of the consequences of parental divorce on children, but empirically, the evidence is scant. Strohschein's (2005) analysis found no gender differences in the effects of parental divorce on measures of mental health among children between the ages of 4 and 11. A series of longitudinal analyses by Sun (2001; Sun & Li, 2002) found no evidence of gender differences in the effects of marital disruption among children who were in high school when their parents divorced. Meta-analyses by Amato (2001; Amato & Keith, 1991) yielded only modest evidence of gender differences in the consequences of marital disruption on children. Morrison and Cherlin (1995) examined the consequences of parental divorce on behavior problems and two measures of achievement in reading. They found no significant effects on girls' well-being and found negative effects averaging one third of a standard deviation on measures of boys' well-being.

Analyzing longitudinal data and examining a wide range of outcomes, Furstenberg and Teitler (1994) identified only a few instances in which effects were more pronounced for one gender than the other. For example, parental separation exerted stronger effects on girls' life satisfaction and boys' substance abuse. But the overall pattern of findings across several outcomes led them to conclude that parental divorce has similar consequences for the well-being of boys and girls.

Variations by children's age at time of divorce. Amato's (2001) meta-analysis reported that there was not much evidence that children's age at the time of parental divorce is an important predictor of their adjustment. Consistent with this conclusion, Furstenberg and Teitler (1994) found no support that children's age at the time of their parents' separation served as a moderator of the effects of divorce on their well-being. However, results from a prospective study suggest otherwise. Ellis et al. (2003)

found that, in both the United States and New Zealand, there was an inverse relationship between the timing of "father absence" (for whatever reason) and the probability of early sexual activity and adolescent pregnancy. The study examined father absence broadly and did not report separate analyses for children who experienced parental divorce, but the results suggest a negative linear relationship between children's age at the time of parental absence and elevated risks of early sexual activity and teenage pregnancy.

◊ NOT ALL OUTCOMES ARE NEGATIVE: RESILIENCE AND MATURATION FOLLOWING PARENTAL DIVORCE

Although there are a number of negative effects of divorce, there are also a number of positive outcomes that may follow divorce. Even with respect to the negative effects of divorce, there is evidence that these effects are short-lived and that most children and young adults return to their predivorce level of functioning within 2 to 3 years following the divorce. Some scholars attribute this pattern to a stress relief hypothesis whereby children's mental health improves after they are removed from an environment characterized by high levels of parental conflict, hostility, and abuse (Amato, Loomis, & Booth, 1995; Jekielek, 1998; Strohschein, 2005; Wheaton, 1990). For example, Sun's (2001) analysis of family environments prior to and following divorce found a pervasive pattern of dysfunction in predisrupted families. Compared with families in which parents would remain married over the course of the study, families in which the parents would later divorce were characterized by worse interparental and parent–child relationships, less parental involvement in children's activities, lower expectations for children, and worse child outcomes. In another study, Strohschein (2005) documented that, even before parental divorce, children whose parents would later divorce had higher levels of anxiety, depression, and antisocial behavior than their peers in families in which parents would remain married.

Longitudinal studies following families through the divorce process demonstrate that both children and parents have the most difficulties during the period when parents separate physically and for the next 1 to 2 years, but then, depending on the adjustment dimension in question, they are often resilient in returning to their previous levels of functioning. Sun and Li (2002) used the National Educational Longitudinal Study data set to trace changes in adolescent well-being across four time points over the span from 3 years prior to divorce to 3 years following divorce. They found that among adolescents whose parents divorced, indicators of academic performance exhibited a continuous and linear decline. However, self-report measures of educational aspirations, self-esteem, and locus of control were characterized by a U-shaped pattern whereby the lowest levels occurred during the divorce, after which levels rebounded to predivorce levels. Applying a process-oriented approach and growth curve modeling to track a national sample of Canadian children, Strohschein (2005) observed that among younger children (ages 4–7 at the beginning of the study), mean levels of anxiety and depression increased over the 4 years of the study, whereas mean levels of antisocial behavior declined. Importantly, Strohschein also noted substantial variation in children's rate of change over time. Although considerably more research is needed to understand children's long-term adjustment to divorce, preliminary evidence suggests that some children may experience stress relief and that they may be more resilient in some domains than others. Perhaps divorce initiates a downward behavioral spiral in academic achievement that is difficult to reverse, whereas divorce has only a short-term effect on psychological adjustment, including internalizing and externalizing behaviors.

Viewed in the aggregate, research suggests that approximately 10% of children with continuously married parents exhibit serious behavior problems, compared with 20% to 25% of children with divorced parents (Hetherington & Kelly, 2002). While this may seem to be a large difference, note that the vast majority of children in both groups are considered to be well-adjusted. Expressed differently, there is substantial overlap in the distribution of well-being scores of children with divorced and nondivorced parents (Amato, 2003). For example, Amato (2003) found that when children who have experienced parental divorce are followed into adulthood, 90% have levels of well-being comparable to their peers with continuously married parents. Such findings further support the idea that children are resilient in that they bounce back relatively quickly from an upsetting event, such as divorce.

Support for the idea that children are resilient to the effects of divorce also comes from the children themselves. Harvey and Fine (2004), in a qualitative analysis, gathered accounts of the divorce experience from thousands of college students whose parents divorced earlier in their lives. A consistent theme in their stories about their experiences was that they managed to cope well in the face of upsetting circumstances and that their adjustment improved over time.

There is also evidence that divorce may have some positive, growth-inducing effects. Research has suggested that the experience of divorce may help children mature more quickly and may assist them in learning some relationship skills and life management skills (e.g., independence, decision making, empathy, understanding, compassion, and tolerance) (Arditti, 1999; Tashiro et al., 2006). Meta-analyses find that, in comparison to children living with first-married parents, children who have experienced parental divorce report more positive mother–child (Kunz, 2001; Reifman et al., 2001) and sibling relationships (Kunz, 2001). Following parental divorce, young adults may have more realistic expectations about romantic relationships, may have an enhanced ability to empathize with their parents and others experiencing difficult circumstances, and may have clearer and more carefully thought out life goals than those whose parents did not divorce. Thus, divorce is not a uniformly negative experience. Negative effects tend to diminish over time, and, for most children, there are some often overlooked positive or maturational effects as well.

☙ CONCLUSIONS

Following parental divorce, most children experience somewhat diminished levels of academic performance, increases in both internalizing and externalizing behaviors, and a higher likelihood of engaging in teen sexual activity. In this chapter, we have reviewed evidence that these group averages mask considerable variability in children's responses to their parents' divorce, including sizable percentages of children for whom functioning improves following parental divorce. We have also documented that, in many cases, children's postdivorce maladjustment can be traced to poor functioning during the period leading up to their parents' separation and divorce. One factor contributing to variation in children's postdivorce outcomes is significant variation in predisruption and postdisruption family processes. In the next chapter, we direct our attention to families that have experienced multiple transitions in family structure.

9

Adults' and Children's Experience of Multiple Family Structure Transitions

F or many families, divorce marks yet another change in a series of changes in family structure. Postdivorce family trajectories take many forms as most formerly married adults enter into new intimate relationships, a rapidly increasing proportion of divorced adults cohabit with a partner or a series of partners, many remarry (often following cohabitation), and a majority of second (and higher order) remarriages end in redivorce. Likewise, for many children, parental divorce signals the first of several family structure transitions as parents enter and exit the household with the formation and dissolution of each cohabiting and remarital relationship. In this chapter, we review our knowledge base regarding how adults and children experience the multiple transitions that precede and follow divorce and the consequences these transitions have for family members' adjustment.

⑊ PREVALENCE OF MULTIPLE FAMILY STRUCTURE TRANSITIONS

As discussed earlier (see Chapter 2), we use the term *family transitions* to refer to changes in family structure, marital status, or household living arrangements that mark the beginning or the termination of cohabiting, marital, or remarital relationships. Applying our Divorce Variation and Fluidity Model (DVFM), we focus attention here on family structure trajectories, or sequences of family structure transitions that typically begin long before divorce. These family structure transitions are quite common. As children age, the probability increases that they will experience family structure change, as does the probability they will experience multiple family transitions. Cavanagh and Huston (2008) found that more than one third of children in the National Institute of Child Health and Development (NICHD) Study of Early Child Care and Youth Development experienced at least one family structure change by the end of fourth grade; nearly one in four experienced two or more transitions. Estimates from the National Longitudinal Study of Adolescent Health indicate that 40% of youth in Grades 7 through 12 have experienced at least one transition in which a parent or a parent's romantic partner moved into or out of the household (Cavanagh, Crissey, & Raley, 2008). In this section, we review what we know about cohabitation, remarriage, and redivorce rates—all of which are family structure transitions that children and adults experience. When family members experience more than one of these events or processes, they have had multiple family structure transitions.

Cohabitation. With dramatic increases in cohabitation rates in recent years (Bumpass & Lu, 2000), a significant percentage of adults experience partnership transitions prior to marriage. Estimates from national probability samples indicate a high incidence of cohabitation throughout the life course. Stewart, Manning, and Smock (2003) found that 21% of currently single men in the United States reported at least one cohabiting relationship. Teachman (2008) examined cohabitation histories among women who were married at least twice and reported that 11% cohabited only with their first husband, 37% cohabited only with their second husband, and 23% cohabited with both husbands. Smaller percentages of women cohabited prior to marriage with someone other than their first husband (3%) or second husband (9%). Thus, Teachman's (2008) results suggest that the vast majority of these women cohabited at least once before marriage. Another study indicated that among the remarried, 39% cohabited with their remarried spouse and 11% cohabited with other partners (Xu, Hudspeth, & Bartkowski, 2006). Sharp increases in cohabitation have fueled transitions not only for adults, but also for children, who are involved in 41% of cohabiting unions (Casper & Bianchi, 2002).

An estimated 2.5 million unmarried couples live with at least one biological child of either partner (U.S. Census Bureau, 2008).

Cohabiting unions tend to be less stable than marital unions in that they are typically of shorter duration and are more likely than either married families or noncohabiting single-mother families to have subsequent transitions (Bumpass & Lu, 2000; Manning, Smock, & Majumdar, 2004; Raley & Wildsmith, 2004). Recent longitudinal data from the Fragile Families and Child Wellbeing Study indicate that nearly half of children born to cohabiting mothers experienced at least one transition in their mothers' partnership status by age 3, and nearly 10% experienced three or more transitions in their first 3 years (Osborne, Manning, & Smock, 2007; Osborne & McLanahan, 2007). Extending prior work by expanding the definition of partnership instability to include dating relationships, Osborne and McLanahan studied noncohabiting mothers (i.e., single mothers who either were not romantically involved with the child's biological father or were romantically involved with him but did not live with him) and found a substantially higher frequency of multiple transitions among these families: More than 40% of children born to noncohabiting mothers experienced two or more transitions in their mothers' partnerships by age 3. Raley and Wildsmith (2004) analyzed the National Survey of Family Growth and found that taking into account cohabitation histories increased the percentages of children who experienced family instability through age 12 by 30% for White children and more than 100% for Black children.

Remarriage. Remarriage, often related to stepfamily formation, represents an additional family structure transition for both adults and children. In the United States, the vast majority (roughly 85%) of those who divorce remarry (Kreider & Fields, 2002), although remarriage rates are lower for Blacks and Hispanics than for Whites (Teachman, Tedrow, & Crowder, 2000) and are somewhat lower for women than men. Remarriage typically occurs quickly: Following a first divorce, the median length of time until remarriage is 3 years (Kreider & Fields, 2002).

Many of those who remarry (and others who cohabit) form stepfamilies involving children from a combination of prior and current relationships. For women, having children from previous relationships is associated with an increased chance of a second or subsequent marriage ending in divorce (Bramlett & Mosher, 2002; Teachman, 2008). Postdivorce cohabitation, either with a future spouse or with multiple partners, is related to lower levels of remarital quality and a higher probability of redivorce (Xu et al., 2006).

Redivorce. Further family structure transitions ensue for the 50% to 60% of remarried individuals (and their children) whose second or higher order marriage ends in redivorce (Bramlett & Mosher, 2002; Ganong et al., 2006). This rate is somewhat higher than the comparable rate for first marriages and indicates that the divorce of a first marriage often leads to an increasing chance of subsequent transitions.

⋙ MULTIPLE FAMILY TRANSITIONS AND ADULTS' AND CHILDREN'S ADJUSTMENT

In this section, we examine the consequences of multiple transitions for both adults' and children's well-being. As will be clear from the discussion below, there has been considerably more attention devoted to the effects of multiple family transitions on children than adults.

Adults. Given the relatively high divorce rates for first and subsequent marriages, multiple divorces are quite common. Demographic data suggest that approximately 17% of adults experience two or more divorces (Amato, 2004). Brody, Neubaum, and Forehand (1988) conducted a thorough review of the literature related to the effects that three or more marriages have on both children and adults, coining the term *serial marriers* for adults who have been married three or more times as a result of multiple divorces. Brody et al. argued that serial marriers were at risk for adjustment problems because they had dysfunctional personality characteristics (e.g., impulsivity, sensation seeking), because they had unrealistic expectations of marriage, because they did not have good conflict resolution skills, because they had numerous stressors stemming from the social stigma attached to people who have married multiple times, and because they had a higher likelihood of divorcing again. Although they found empirical support for this claim, the evidence was based on just a few limited studies. Kurdek (1990), with a more representative sample of newlywed couples, found that wives with a history of multiple divorces had higher levels of psychoticism, distress, and anxiety than did wives with zero or one previous divorce, although the effects were modest in size. No divorce history effects were found for husbands. In one of the very few recent studies, Cavanagh and Huston (2006) showed that maternal depression was positively related to the number of family transitions (i.e., marriage, divorce, cohabitation, singlehood) experienced before the mothers' children reached kindergarten, and perhaps more important, the rate of increase in depression also rose as the number of family transitions increased. Thus, family transitions were not only related to higher levels of depression, but also to higher rates of increase in depression.

Thus, the general conclusion is that multiple family structure transitions have modest detrimental effects for women, and perhaps for men, but these negative consequences for adults are smaller in magnitude than are the comparable effects for children (see below). Perhaps the effects on adults are smaller because adults (to varying degrees) choose to make these transitions, whereas children's transitions are often decided for them; because many adults have more sophisticated and effective coping skills than children; and/or because some adults may become more accustomed to divorce stressors (and presumably are less affected by them) with each subsequent divorce.

Children. For children, each family structure transition can be emotionally stressful, so there is the potential that the cumulative effect of multiple transitions across childhood and adolescence may be quite harmful. When parents and their romantic partners move into and out of the household, there are disruptions in adult sources of support, nurturance, supervision, and discipline. Changes in parenting behaviors, family routines, and emotional attachments are often accompanied by changes in residences, schools, neighborhoods, and peer groups. In addition, the impact of family structure transitions on the family's economic resources may be positive or negative depending on the nature of the transition: Family income typically declines when a parent exits the household, but often increases when an additional wage-earner enters the household (Sayer, 2006).

As shown in Figure 2.1, in the presence of protective factors, children may be resilient to one family structure transition, such as parental divorce. Evidence reviewed in Chapter 8 demonstrates that 75% to 80% of children are functioning in the normal range of adjustment within 2 to 3 years following divorce. Subsequent transitions, however, particularly if they occur with rapidity, may introduce additional stressors and may seriously compromise children's ability to be resilient. For example, analyses of data from three waves of the Fragile Families Study found that the frequency of mothers' partnership transitions was associated with increases in children's aggressive and anxious/depressive behavior at age 3 (Osborne & McLanahan, 2007). Although a single partnership change was associated with only a modest detrimental effect (an effect size of 0.09 standard deviations for each outcome), the effects were additive, resulting in large effects for children who experienced multiple transitions, and there were no threshold effects (i.e., there did not seem to be a maximum number of family structure transitions beyond which no further negative effects were noted). Further, the pattern of accumulating effects of multiple transitions was obtained across White, Black, and Hispanic children.

Mechanisms underlying the effects of family structure transitions on children's outcomes. Several mechanisms may explain the effect of family structure transitions on children's outcomes—a link that we included in the DVFM in Figure 2.1. The most common, and perhaps the broadest, explanation is that family structure transitions, including divorce and remarriage, evoke stress for all family members. Substantial evidence indicates that family transitions are associated with elevated stress, diminished parenting effectiveness, and lower levels of adult and child adjustment (Amato, 2000; Coleman, Ganong, & Fine, 2000; Hetherington, Bridges, & Insabella, 1998).

Recent longitudinal studies provide evidence consistent with a stress explanation by linking the frequency of family structure transitions with reduced child well-being. For example, Heard's (2007) examination of the National Longitudinal Study of Adolescent Health found that the number of family structure changes across childhood was related to lower grade point averages and college expectations, as well as a higher number of school suspensions in adolescence. Other studies measuring the frequency of family structure transitions over time corroborate deleterious consequences for children's anxiety-depression (Osborne & McLanahan, 2007), social adjustment (Cavanagh & Huston, 2008), aggression and behavior problems (Ackerman, Kogos, Youngstrom, Schoff, & Izard, 1999; Capaldi & Patterson, 1991; Cavanagh & Huston, 2006, 2008; Fomby & Cherlin, 2007), earlier onset of sexual activity (Capaldi, Crosby, & Stoolmiller, 1996; Wu & Thomson, 2001), and a greater likelihood of premarital childbearing (Wu & Martinson, 1993). Consequences appear to persist into adulthood, with those who experienced more family transitions during childhood generally attaining less education, having less prestigious jobs, and earning less income (Sun & Li, 2008). However, there is no evidence that the effect of multiple transitions in childhood living arrangements extends to an increased risk of divorce as adults (Teachman, 2002).

The growing research literature on children's experience of multiple family structure transitions generally supports a stress explanation for harmful consequences, but the evidence is not uniform and the exact mechanisms for these effects are not yet clear. In support of a stress explanation, Osborne and McLanahan (2007) demonstrated that maternal stress was a significant mediator of the effect of family transitions on children's anxiety-depression in early childhood. In another study designed to test mechanisms underlying the influence of family structure instability, Fomby and Cherlin (2007) found some evidence suggesting a causal relationship between number of transitions and children's behavioral problems in middle childhood and early adolescence. On the other hand, Carlson and Corcoran (2001) studied children with different family structure histories in the National Longitudinal Study of Youth and presented evidence challenging the stress hypothesis. They found that among children ages 7 to 10, the highest levels of behavior problems and lowest cognitive development scores were observed among children living in continuous single-parent families who, by definition, had not experienced any family structure transitions. In this case, these children's poorer outcomes may be due to stresses inherent in having only one adult to perform household and childcare labor and having few socioeconomic resources—factors that may outweigh the beneficial impact of not having any family structure transitions.

It is also likely that stress exerts effects indirectly through altered family processes. A number of studies suggest that one mechanism through which family structure transitions influence children's adjustment is inconsistent parenting and expectations. The general idea is that the stressful nature of forming or dissolving intimate relationships, and of family members moving into or out of the household, makes it more difficult for parents (whether residential, nonresidential, biological, or nonbiological) to be as consistent in supporting, monitoring, and disciplining children as they would be without the stresses associated with relationship disruptions. Empirical evidence supports this proposition, indicating that parenting effectiveness is a significant mediator of the relationship between number of family structure transitions and child outcomes (Martinez & Forgatch, 2002; Osborne & McLanahan, 2007).

Another explanation, derived from life-course theory, emphasizes the cumulation of disadvantages experienced across childhood and adolescence when there are multiple changes in children's living arrangements. Elder (1998, p. 6) argues that "a concatenation of negative events and influences" can have long-term consequences for life-course trajectories and developmental outcomes. According to this view, the stresses associated with parents and other adults moving in and out of the household are compounded by changes in parenting behaviors, residence, schools, peer networks, and economic resources. Further, these disruptions and misfortunes have cumulative effects (Osborne & McLanahan, 2007), making it difficult for some children to mobilize the personal and social resources to offset the effects of diverse stressors, new expectations, and lost opportunities. Much of the empirical evidence demonstrating an association between number of family structure transitions and children's adjustment problems, summarized above, can also be interpreted as support for a life-course perspective that emphasizes the accumulation of disadvantages and specifies some of the mechanisms through which stress influences family processes and child adjustment. Further support for the life-course perspective was provided by Heard (2007), who found that the duration of time children spent in any family arrangements other than two-original-parent families (e.g., cohabiting mother-stepfather families, single father, or single mother families) was associated with lower grade point averages among adolescents. Cavanagh et al. (2008) observed that their measure of cumulative family instability was associated with an increased probability of adolescents forming romantic relationships; each family structure transition was associated with a 13% increase in the odds of the adolescent establishing a romantic union. The researchers suggest that two processes may be operating: Family instability and reduced monitoring provide greater opportunities for adolescents to pursue romantic relationships, and at the same time, family disruption and tension may provide motivation for adolescents to seek romantic relationships and the comfort they might provide.

In contrast to explanations emphasizing the causal influences of stress, inconsistent parenting, or cumulative disadvantages, a selection perspective posits that individuals with certain characteristics (e.g., socially undesirable attributes or serious psychological problems) are more likely than others to have difficulty maintaining intimate partnerships and thus are prone to experience more relationship transitions. Further, parents' cognitive and personality characteristics influence their parenting behaviors, and these characteristics may be transmitted to their children through a combination of environmental (e.g., parenting behaviors) and genetic mechanisms. Thus, parents' antecedent characteristics may serve as "third variables" that cause both family disruptions and child-adjustment problems. There is modest empirical support for this explanation. Osborne and McLanahan's (2007) investigation of partnership transitions found that maternal stress and ineffective parenting fully and independently mediated the effects of partnership transitions on child behavior. Fomby and

Cherlin (2007) found that the relationship between the number of family structure transitions and children's cognitive achievement was attenuated when mothers' prior characteristics were examined, and they cautiously interpret their pattern of findings as providing partial support for a selection perspective.

Other explanations are possible, as well, for the link between multiple family structure transitions and children's (mal)adjustment. Osborne and McLanahan (2007) advance a reverse causation argument, which asserts that children's behavior problems create stress for parents, undermine parental adjustment, and weaken parents' marital and cohabiting relationships. It is likely, indeed probable, that each of these mechanisms—elevated stress, inconsistent parenting, cumulative disadvantages, selection, and reverse causation—operates to some degree in most families that experience serial family structure transitions. In addition, the type and timing of each transition may be consequential, although the empirical evidence relating to these concepts is limited. Regarding type of transition, there are some preliminary indications that entrances of adults into the household (typically male cohabiting partners or stepfathers) are more disruptive than exits (Fomby & Cherlin, 2007; Heard, 2007). Analyses of the National Longitudinal Study of Adolescent Health indicated that the transition from a two-parent family to a single-parent family was unrelated to adolescent well-being (Brown, 2006; Videon, 2002), but a transition from single-parent family to a cohabiting stepfamily was harmful (Brown, 2006).

Evidence regarding the effects of the timing of family structure transitions is mixed, and there is a dire need for more work on this topic. Some research and theory suggest stronger influences of family transitions in early childhood (Heard, 2007; Rimm-Kaufman & Pianta, 2000), whereas other studies suggest that transitions during middle childhood and adolescence are more problematic (Cavanagh et al., 2008; McLanahan & Sandefur, 1994). The outcome of interest is also important, and some child outcomes may be more adversely affected by earlier transitions, while other outcomes are more adversely affected by later transitions (Lansford et al., 2006). Research is needed that examines the number, type, and timing of family structure transitions that occur over the course of childhood and adolescence, as well as the duration of time spent in specific family types. Many family structure trajectories are characterized by entrances and exits of adults in early childhood, subsequent transitions in middle childhood, and further changes in adolescence. It will be important for future research to identify how particular aspects of family structure history relate to specific dimensions of child and adolescent adjustment.

⚡ VARIATION IN CHILDREN'S ADJUSTMENT TO MULTIPLE PARENTING TRANSITIONS

The recent attention devoted to investigating family structure trajectories is impressive and has yielded valuable insights regarding children's adjustment to family structure transitions. Researchers know very little, however, regarding variation in children's adjustment to multiple parenting transitions. For example, how does the influence of family structure instability vary by gender and race-ethnicity? With respect to gender, one study (Cavanagh & Huston, 2008) found that the negative impact of family instability on children's social development at the end of elementary school (including increases in loneliness and externalizing behaviors and decreases in peer competency) was stronger for boys. Another study (Heard, 2007) suggests that parents' gender is important, as it found that mother transitions had stronger effects than father transitions. Clearly much more research is needed to explore how the gender of both parents and children interacts with the type, timing, and frequency of family transitions to alter family processes (e.g., parenting behaviors) and thus influence child adjustment.

A second social structural dimension likely to be associated with children's adjustment to family structure transitions is race-ethnicity. As we described above, the nature of childhood living arrangements and family structure trajectories is quite different for many Black and Hispanic children than it is for most White children. In the aggregate, Black children experience the most family structure transitions (Raley & Wildsmith, 2004), and Black and Hispanic children experience more transitions involving cohabitation (Bumpass & Lu, 2000; Raley & Wildsmith, 2004) and fewer transitions involving divorce and remarriage (Teachman et al., 2000). Yet the available empirical evidence suggests that the number of transitions in childhood family structure exerts a stronger influence on adjustment among White children than among Black or Mexican-origin children (Fomby & Cherlin, 2007; Wu & Thomson, 2001). Similar findings have been obtained in other studies that have indicated weak relationships or no association between family structure and children's outcomes in Black and Latino families (Dunifon & Kowaleski-Jones, 2002; Foster & Kalil, 2007). It will be important for future work to investigate how extended and multigenerational families provide contexts in which racial and ethnic minority families experience and can be resilient to family disruption and reformation, and to identify the family processes and other mechanisms responsible for adult and child adjustment.

〰 CONCLUSIONS

The life-course trajectories of American families are now much more likely than in the past to include multiple transitions in family structure, including the formation and dissolution of cohabiting, marital, and remarital relationships, as well as serial changes in parenting arrangements as parents and their partners move in and out of the household. Most research on family structure and child adjustment has relied on static measures of children's living arrangements at one point in time and average (or mean) scores of child outcomes across family types. Although useful, as noted earlier in Chapter 3, such studies confound the effects of family structure (i.e., the type of family in which the child is currently living) with those of family transitions (i.e., the disruptions and stresses associated with each of the family-parenting transitions that the child has experienced). The smaller body of work focusing on the frequency of family transitions across time, reviewed in this chapter, indicates that children, and adults to a lesser extent, become more vulnerable with each family structure transition they experience. Now that it has been established that there is such a link, the critical task for future research is to identify the mechanisms through which family transitions impact parenting behavior, adult adjustment, and child adjustment, including the specification of contextual characteristics such as gender and race-ethnicity that may moderate these influences.

PART III

Future Directions

10

Implications
and Conclusions

Previous chapters have provided an aerial view of the landscape of divorce. Our dynamic theoretical model, the Divorce Variation and Fluidity Model (DVFM) introduced in Chapter 2, presented our conceptualization of how an array of variables affects three different aspects of the divorce experience: average-mean level of adjustment, variability in adjustment, and fluidity in adjustment over time. Chapter 3 described quantitative and qualitative methods that have been used and that could be used to test our theoretical model (as well as other models) and to extend the rich knowledge base on divorce and its aftermath. Using the theoretical and methodological background provided in the first 3 chapters, Chapters 4 through 9 provided a focused and tailored review of a number of different aspects of the divorce information base, including predisruption, during disruption, and postdisruption experiences and outcomes for both adults and children. We depict the reviews in these six chapters as focused and tailored because, although we describe mean differences in outcomes among adults and children from various family structure groups, we place greater emphasis on variability and fluidity.

In this chapter, we use the theoretical, methodological, and substantive foundations laid in the first nine chapters to suggest where divorce scholars and practitioners need to direct their future efforts. To bring closure to the book, we discuss implications of our analysis for theory construction, research, practice, and policy. More specifically, in the sections that follow we describe implications for a) further development and refinement of our dynamic model of divorce; b) subsequent research on divorce, including suggestions for methodological approaches and content areas in particular need of study; c) helping those who are experiencing or who have experienced divorce; and d) helping policy become more sensitive to the plight of those who have been or may eventually be touched by divorce.

∥∥ THEORETICAL DEVELOPMENT

We concur with an esteemed group of divorce scholars (e.g., Ahrons, Amato, Duck, Emery, Hetherington, and Kitson) who have argued that divorce needs to be viewed as a long and dynamic process rather than as a single event. In this book, we have extended the notion that divorce is a dynamic process to highlight the importance of variability and fluidity in experiences and outcomes over time.

More theoretical work needs to be done to flesh out the mechanisms involved in explaining mean outcome levels, variability in outcomes, and fluidity in outcomes. Clearly, previous work has focused primarily, or even exclusively, on predicting mean levels of adjustment. Our model, however, goes beyond that in its attempt to identify predictors of variability and fluidity in adjustment. An example or two may help to clarify the possible mechanisms involved. The quality of predisruption and postdisruption parenting has been identified as a predictor of children's adjustment following divorce (Amato, 2000; Barber & Demo, 2006; Hetherington & Kelly, 2002). High quality parenting is related to better child outcomes.

We extend this well-established finding, however, to propose that the quality of parenting may also be related to variability and fluidity in adjustment. One possible working hypothesis is that there will be less variability in adjustment for groups of children who experience high quality parenting relative to those who experience less effective parenting. With high quality parenting, there is relatively less opportunity for an array of other factors to negatively influence children's adjustment. In other words, effective parenting is so potent a factor in helping children function well that it may lead to less variability in children's functional levels. By contrast, when children are ineffectively parented, particularly when they are not adequately supervised or are neglected, there is more opportunity for other factors to sway children in a negative direction. Thus, because there are a greater number of other factors that can play an important role in determining children's adjustment, we might expect that there would be more variability in children's outcomes when parenting has been inadequate. Our working hypothesis, therefore, is based on the notion that a potent and effective force—effective parenting in this case—will not only lead to better outcomes for children but will also leave less room for other factors to negatively influence children, which will lower variability among groups of children who are effectively parented.

How might the quality of parenting affect the fluidity of children's adjustment to divorce? As is consistent with empirical evidence reviewed elsewhere in the book, we propose that higher quality parenting will be related to a quicker recovery to baseline levels of functioning. In other words, as reflected in the DVFM, effective parenting can be viewed as a factor that promotes resiliency, which operationally means that children whose adjustment levels have suffered during and following parental divorce would return to their previous levels of functioning more quickly to the extent that they were parented well.

At a more general level, we propose that any factor that facilitates adults' and children's adjustment (e.g., effective parenting, coping skills, social support, self-esteem) will tend to reduce variability in adjustment and increase the rate at which individuals return to their baseline level of functioning (or even surpass their baseline level of functioning) following divorce (i.e., fluidity). For example, adults with good coping skills and high levels of social support are not only likely to adjust better to the divorce process, but are also likely to have less variability in adjustment levels and to return more rapidly to their previous levels of functioning. Lower levels of social support and poorer coping skills leave more room for other factors to influence the adjustment process and should therefore lead to greater variability in adjustment and slower returns to previous levels of functioning. Thus, our theoretical proposal is that the presence of risk factors is likely to increase variability and, consistent with empirical evidence, lengthen the amount of time required to return to predivorce levels of functioning.

Finally, we propose that conceptual attention needs to be directed to a number of related constructs in this literature—family transition, family instability, parenting transition, family structure, and family composition. One of the conceptual issues involved in defining these constructs is whether or not a transition needs to be a legal transition. In other words, are transitions marked only by changes in legal status, such as marriage or divorce, or do they include nonlegal changes, such as beginning or discontinuing cohabitation with a romantic partner, changes in residence, or changes in the size and composition of a social support system? For research purposes, it is easier to track legal transitions, and this partially explains why previous investigators have tended to consider marriage and divorce as the markers of change (e.g., Kurdek & Fine, 1994; Kurdek et al., 1994). However, conceptually, all partnership changes, regardless of whether or not they are tracked by legal agreements, may be viewed as transitions that impact the experiences and adjustment of children and adults. Indeed, recent work has taken a broader view of family transitions to include not only cohabitation transitions, but also transitions in dating relationships (see Osborne & McLanahan, 2007).

A second issue involves whether these constructs are considered to be family-level or individual-level variables. For example, consider a family consisting of two children-stepchildren from one of the spouse's previous marriages and two "mutual" children from the present marriage. From the perspective of the two mutual children, especially if the two older children are now living outside of their family home, they are in a nuclear family because they are living with both of their biological parents. From the perspective of the two older children-stepchildren, this family is appropriately labeled as a stepfamily. From a family-level perspective, a family scholar would likely classify this family as a stepfamily because the parents are in a remarriage and because of the presence of stepchildren. Scholars need to explicitly describe whether they are defining relevant terms at the individual or family level. Ideally, the field should attempt to reach consensual definitions, including addressing the issue of whether the construct refers to an individual construct or a family construct. Some scholars have used the term *family structure* to refer to the family-level construct, whereas others use the term *family composition* to refer to the individual-level construct (Demo et al., 2005).

A third issue involves whether or not the family unit should consist of just those individuals living in the household or whether it should also include family members living in multiple households. Family structure and family composition, for example, are often used to refer to those members living in the family residence; when family members in other residences are considered, they are often identified as living in some variant of an extended family household. We prefer the more inclusive definition that includes all family members regardless of which household they live in, but even more important, we encourage researchers to push for consensus regarding how these definitions consider and address the household issue.

〽 RESEARCH IMPLICATIONS

Below, we present research implications stemming from the DVFM. First, we review methodological implications, and then we present some suggestions for topics that we believe merit additional inquiry.

Methodological implications. Our first implication is not a novel or unique one, and in fact, it has been noted by hundreds if not thousands of scholars: Both quantitative and qualitative methods are essential in the study of divorce because they enrich and complement each other. This plea warrants additional attention here because most of the evidence discussed in this book has been obtained from quantitative methods. We believe that qualitative work is essential in providing depth to our understanding of how individuals and families experience the divorce process. Some aspects of the divorce process—such as how individuals assign meaning to divorce-related events—do not easily lend themselves to quantitative study. Qualitative methods, particularly in-depth interviewing, can tap into divorced individuals' narratives of the ebbs and flows (i.e., fluidity) of their divorce-related experiences and the meanings that they assign to critical events as they traverse the divorce process.

Second, it is critical that researchers employ longitudinal designs to track fluidity and changes over time. In Chapter 3, we argued that fluidity and change in divorce-related experiences are best studied prospectively (i.e., assessing participants at multiple times before, during, and after marital disruption), although retrospective research designs (i.e., asking participants at one point in time to reflect on their experiences in the past) can also provide useful information. Retrospective designs are somewhat useful because change can be inferred from data on participants' reported experiences at different points in time. Such designs are limited, however, because of the possibility of social desirability responding (i.e., individuals giving what they believe to be the socially acceptable response) and less than accurate recall. As a result, prospective designs are generally superior when studying a long-term process and should become the default when designing divorce-related studies. Such studies should begin before the legal divorce occurs and, ideally, before family disruption begins. Further, investigations need to extend beyond the typical 1 to 4 years after the divorce. Relatively few studies have followed participants beyond 5 years, with the notable exceptions of studies by Ahrons,

Hetherington, and Wallerstein. We also need to note that although some of the existing longitudinal data sets have provided rich information on family structure histories, they provide relatively less insight into such family processes as parenting behaviors, interparental conflict, and sibling interactions. With few exceptions, longitudinal data on family processes have not been gathered.

Third, there is a statistical implication arising from the call for even greater use of long-term longitudinal studies—a need to use growth curve analyses and hierarchical linear modeling, when the data permit, to further our understanding of how changes in predictor variables (those to the left and center in Figure 2.1) are related to changes in adults' and children's adjustment (the boxes to the far right in Figure 2.1). Further, researchers need to assess whether their data might best be characterized by nonlinear growth trajectories in addition to considering whether there are linear changes over time. In other words, given our sense that the divorce process unfolds in anything but a straightforward linear pattern and that it is characterized by frequent ebbs and flows, we should routinely test whether curvilinear trajectories characterize individuals' changes over time.

Finally, as reflected on the far right side of Figure 2.1, we believe that researchers need to begin to think of variability as a dependent variable in future research. In conducting such analyses, it is important to take into consideration the nature of variability scores—that is, variability characterizes groups of scores rather than being a characteristic possessed by each participant in a study. We acknowledge that there is intra-individual variability over time, which we have referred to throughout this book as fluidity, but our point here refers not to change over time, but to scores at only one time point. Thus, to assess the extent to which a predictor variable is related to variability in some divorce-related outcome, groups of individuals need to be compared in terms of their level of variability. For example, the simplest test of the hypothesis posed earlier in this chapter—that more effective parenting will be related to less variability in child outcomes—would be to compare the standard deviations of outcome measures for a group of children that has been assessed as receiving high quality parenting with the standard deviations of a group that has been identified as receiving poorer quality parenting. If the high quality parenting group has smaller standard deviations than the poorer quality group, the hypothesis would be supported. To conduct inferential statistical comparisons, one could compare variability scores from a sufficiently large number of high quality parenting groups with those from a number of poorer quality parenting groups. If there were a statistically significant difference in the expected direction, the hypothesis would receive greater support than merely comparing two groups of children.

Topics needing scholarly attention. Topics warranting additional study include, first, whether the frequency of family transitions (see above for a discussion of issues involved in defining this construct) is related to mean levels, variability in, and the fluidity of children's and adults' adjustment. Chapter 9 presented research that examined how multiple transitions are experienced by those who have gone through divorce, but such studies have only touched the surface of what we need to know. For example, it would be helpful to explore if subsequent divorces are more stressful for children and adults than is the first one. On one hand, one might expect that an individual would become increasingly accepting and understanding of the divorce process each time that he or she experiences it. On the other hand, subsequent divorces might be even more stressful because they tax the individuals' coping resources to a greater degree and because they magnify the losses experienced (each divorce carries with it unique losses and challenges).

Another related issue pertains to the relative stressfulness of different types of family transitions. Are positive events such as marriage less stressful than negative events such as divorce? Which factors account for the stressfulness of subsequent transitions? Is the reduced amount of contact with the nonresidential parent the most influential factor in determining children's subsequent stress and adjustment levels? How influential is the decline in socioeconomic resources available to the child and family? Are legal transitions (e.g., marriage and divorce) more or less stressful than nonlegal ones (e.g., cohabitation, separation)? Are changes in the parents' romantic status more influential than other types of changes (e.g., changes in residence, moving into a new school district)?

A third topic worthy of scholarly attention is to study variation (in mean scores and in fluidity over time) in adjustment along key dimensions of diversity, such as race-ethnicity, sexual orientation, socioeconomic status, and gender. As noted elsewhere in the book, we know relatively more about the divorce-related experiences of White, heterosexual, and middle to upper-middle socioeconomic status individuals and families than we do of other individuals and families. Thus, how divorce is experienced by the full range of individuals represented along these dimensions of diversity requires considerable additional study. For example, to flesh out the meaning of some of the demographic differences across various subgroups of individuals (e.g., the lower marriage rate and higher divorce rate of African Americans relative to other racial-ethnic groups; the lower divorce rate of elderly couples), it would be helpful to understand the values and norms, as well as the sociocultural context (see Chapter 4), that underlie family and divorce-related behaviors. In addition, there is a need for within-group studies to identify factors associated with variation in divorce adjustment within specific racial-ethnic, socioeconomic, or other groups (Foster & Kalil, 2007).

A fourth area in need of future research is to empirically test the key paths shown in Figure 2.1, particularly the links between the predictor variables and the variability and fluidity dimensions of adult and child adjustment. In addition, as suggested immediately above, the links need to be studied among the full range of populations and subpopulations affected by divorce.

A fifth topic of study is the similarities and differences between the experience of divorce and the experience of nonmarital relationship dissolution, including heterosexual cohabiting, gay, and lesbian relationships.

Finally, it would be fruitful to further explore how the divorce-related experiences of parents compare with those of adults who have not had children. We know that the presence of children adds stress to the divorce process, but it is not yet clear if this particular stressor is just one of many stressors (e.g., change in social support network, change in residence, change in income level) that add complexity to the process or if having children represents a unique and particularly salient category that leads to very different experiences and adjustment trajectories. To address this, it would be informative to interview adults with and without children regarding how they believe that this variable has affected their experiences and their plans for the future.

⧂ IMPLICATIONS FOR APPLICATION

Practitioners working with divorcing adults or children whose parents are divorcing should not underestimate the extent to which family disruption represents a risk factor for a range of undesirable child (Chapter 8) and adult (Chapter 7) outcomes. At the same time, however, practitioners should be aware that the mean differences between children with divorced and continuously married parents are not large in absolute terms (Amato, 2001). These relatively small differences are illustrative of the diversity of outcomes among children in both groups. The adjustment of children following divorce depends on a variety of factors other than merely the divorce itself, including the level of conflict between parents before and after separation, the quality of parenting from both the residential and nonresidential parent, changes in the standard of living, and the number of additional stressors to which children are exposed, such as moving or changing schools. Depending on the specific constellation of factors around the time of divorce, children may exhibit an improvement in the quality of their functioning, a modest decline in functioning that improves over time, a substantial long-term decline in functioning, or little change. Knowledge of group averages, therefore, cannot predict how a particular child will adjust to family disruption (Amato, 2001).

In this section, we provide recommendations for two types of interventions designed to assist those who are experiencing or have experienced divorce: educational programs for divorcing parents and psychotherapeutic interventions for divorcing or divorced individuals and families. These are probably the most frequently offered interventions, and they vary in their intended populations. Educational programs are preventative in nature and attempt to help parents facilitate their children's adjustment before serious problems arise, whereas psychotherapeutic interventions typically, although not always, take place after problems reach clinical proportions. Each is reviewed in turn, with our recommendations for how to make them more sensitive to the needs of individuals and families.

Educational programs for divorcing parents. Educational programs for divorcing parents are an increasingly common, and even mandated, intervention not only in the United States, but also in other countries, such as in the United Kingdom, Canada, and Australia (Blaisure & Geasler, 2006). Typically, they involve a single 2- or 3-hour session for divorcing parents and focus primarily on teaching parents how to more effectively help their children adjust to divorce, often by encouraging parents to keep their children out of the middle of their continuing conflicts. The first, and obvious, recommendation based on the continuing themes posed throughout the book is that such programs need to be more sensitive to variability and fluidity over time rather than to present information as if the process is experienced in the same manner and with the same trajectories by all adults and children. One implication of this suggestion is that program presenters should transmit information, research findings, and advice in a manner that is consistent with the notion that there are wide variations in divorce-related experiences and outcomes. A second implication is that programs could be developed separately for different subgroups that have clearly differing experiences, needs, and outcomes. For example, because of the variability and fluidity described throughout the book, programs might be developed and offered separately for adults who are experiencing their first divorce versus those who are experiencing their second or later divorce (see Chapter 9), parents of young versus older children, and parents who have just filed for divorce versus those who are filing or responding to motions to modify the original divorce decree.

A second recommendation involves the timing of such educational programs. Such programs are typically offered or mandated very soon after filing for divorce, such as within a month after filing. Research presented earlier in this book suggests that it might be helpful to supplement this early educational experience with, if the population can be identified and recruited, an earlier program that occurs during the family disruption period, but before the actual filing for divorce. Evidence reviewed in Chapter 5 suggests that the process of marital disaffection begins long before the legal divorce, that parenting effectiveness declines in the months and years before marital dissolution, and that the well-being of parents and children suffers as the process of marital disruption unfolds. Further, as described in Chapter 6, identity and security are threatened during the predivorce separation period partly because of changes in routines and rituals. While it would probably not be possible to mandate that spouses or couples attend a predivorce educational or counseling session, programs could be developed and offered (voluntarily) to those who recognize that their relationships are dysfunctional and who acknowledge that they could benefit from some assistance in helping their children adjust to their marital tension and conflict.

Research presented in Chapters 7 and 8 indicates that most, although not all, children and adults return to near their predisruption baseline levels of functioning within 2 to 3 years following the divorce. Thus, it may be helpful to offer an additional educational session or program sometime between the first and second years following the legal divorce to perhaps accelerate the pace of this recovery. Parents will have had a host of divorce-related experiences between the mandated educational session that they attend within a month of filing for divorce and the proposed session 1 or 2 years later. For example, one or both parents may have established new romantic relationships and need to deal with how to integrate their romantic and parenting lives; the parents will have had experience in implementing the parenting plan that was established earlier, including coparenting successes and perhaps failures in working through child support and visitation issues; and parents may have new psychological issues to work through as they continue to develop and refine their narratives of how the relationship and divorce unfolded. Thus, because parents' and their children's needs are likely to be different 1 or 2 years after the divorce than they were immediately after filing for divorce, the proposed session-program may be helpful in addressing these needs.

A final suggestion with respect to the timing of such educational programs is that they need not necessarily be offered based on time-related schedules, but instead on the basis of the occurrence of particularly relevant events. For example, rather than offering (or even mandating) an educational session between the first and second years postdivorce, programs might be offered or even mandated for those who are undergoing specific events known to challenge children's (and parents') adjustment, such as when one parent files a motion to change the original divorce decree, when one parent moves out of state, or when one parent remarries.

Third, to an even greater extent than is currently the case, such programs should have their curricula determined by empirical findings, such as those presented in this book. To whatever extent possible, program developers should attempt to ensure that curricular decisions are guided by results from high quality empirical studies as opposed to unverified suspicions and intuition. For example, it is popular for counselors and educators to herald the virtues of joint physical custody, even though research findings present a more nuanced and cautious picture—a picture suggesting that joint physical custody may be particularly effective when both parents voluntarily choose to enter such an agreement, as opposed to when they are mandated to do so.

Therapists-counselors working with divorced clients. Variability and fluidity are as relevant to therapists and counselors as they are to parent educators. In terms of variability, therapists should become aware of recent findings on people's differing responses to divorce so that they can stress to clients that there is no single uniform divorce experience. This sounds like an obvious suggestion that perhaps need not be mentioned, but two aspects of this implication warrant special attention. First, therapists need to deliberately resist succumbing to the prevailing narrative that divorce has uniformly negative consequences for every adult and child. The research reviewed in this book highlights that there are some adults and children who are not detrimentally affected by divorce, that even those who are negatively affected may benefit in some ways, and that there are even some who may have only positive consequences following divorce. Thus, even though all family members experience divorce as stressful because of the inevitable changes that it precipitates, therapists and counselors need to be open to the possibility that their divorced clients may have benefitted from their divorce experience.

A second way that variability is relevant involves the notion of mediators of divorce effects. In Chapter 8, for example, we reviewed the most widely supported mediators of divorce effects on children, such as interparental conflict, the quality of nonresidential parenting, and loss of socioeconomic resources. The presence of these, and other, empirically supported mediators suggests that the variability in divorce experiences and outcomes is not random, but is systematically related to these mediating variables. Because these mediators have been empirically supported, therapists and counselors can expect that children will function less effectively following divorce to the extent that their parents are engaged in extensive conflict, that they are parented ineffectively, and that they lose considerable financial resources. Of course, clinicians need to temper these expectations with a healthy skepticism given the facts that there are a large number of mediators operative at any given time for any given individual and that all predictions involve some error. Thus, because much of the variability in outcomes is systematic and nonrandom, a key task for future research is to improve the accuracy of divorce-related predictions by identifying more potent mediating (and moderating) effects on divorce outcomes.

With respect to fluidity, therapists need to remain cognizant of the oft-repeated theme in this book that divorce is a lengthy process. If therapists develop treatment plans based on only a static understanding of clients' experience and adjustment, they may underestimate the changes that naturally unfold over time as the process ensues or, even more seriously, may design interventions that could inhibit how quickly children and adults can rebound from the stressors of divorce. For example, consider a therapist who observes that an adult client who has just divorced is quite reluctant to initiate a new romantic relationship. Such a hesitancy and cautiousness is quite common, perhaps even expected, and possibly adaptive in the short term, but if the therapist regards the reluctance to pursue romance as a tendency that is dysfunctional and likely to continue into the future, the therapist may initiate possibly destructive therapeutic strategies such as (prematurely) encouraging the client to make concerted attempts to meet new romantic partners. Thus, clinicians need to be aware of the ebbs and flows that characterize the divorce process.

≫ POLICY IMPLICATIONS

The model presented in Chapter 2 and the research reviewed throughout this book have implications for policy related to divorce. In this chapter, several suggestions are made that stem directly from our theoretical model, empirically established findings, or both. First, does theory and research provide guidance about whether to make divorce easier or more difficult for couples to obtain? It is difficult, if not impossible, to draw objective conclusions regarding this issue without allowing personal values to affect one's recommendations. However, the data do provide some useful guidance. On one hand, the modest negative effects of divorce that have been described throughout the book might suggest that couples should face more barriers in getting a divorce, such as longer waiting periods or required counseling before the divorce. It is possible that children and adults who have experienced divorce might have fared better had they (or their parents) remained married. In addition, some (Popenoe, 1996) have argued that divorce, particularly no-fault divorce, has made it too easy to divorce and that couples can now decide to divorce before they genuinely work to improve their relationship.

On the other hand, many instances of maladjustment, as discussed in Chapters 7 and 8, were present before the divorce occurred, indicating that the divorce per se was not the sole factor leading to later adjustment problems. In addition, there is some evidence that children and adults benefit more from divorce than they would if the alternative were staying in a conflictual, dysfunctional marriage (Amato & Hohmann-Marriott, 2007; Booth & Amato, 2001), again suggesting that it may not be the divorce itself that causes adjustment problems, but rather the conflict and distress associated with a dysfunctional marriage. Finally, our sense, from both research and experience, is that people, especially those with children, do not take divorce lightly. In fact, there is evidence that the presence of children lowers the likelihood of divorce (Emery, 1999), suggesting that some people may delay or avoid divorce for the sake of the children. Because the decision to divorce is often well thought out, it is possible that waiting periods and other barriers may have the unintended side effect of lengthening the amount of time that it takes for family members to return to or to surpass baseline levels of functioning. These other barriers include that the adversarial legal system makes divorce a lengthy, difficult, expensive, stressful, and emotionally draining process, which can only exacerbate any negative effects that the divorce process has on family members.

Clearly, as noted above, there is no objective answer to the question about the ease with which divorce should or could be obtained. How one interprets the literature, the values one has related to family matters, and one's personal experiences with divorce are likely to sway each person one way or the other.

A second policy implication pertains to child support awards. As described in Chapters 7 and 8, financial well-being following divorce is a critical factor in determining how adults and children will adjust to family disruption. Thus, we advocate for measures that increase the chances that children will regularly receive the full amount of child support payments from the nonresidential parent. We support recent measures that have improved compliance to child support awards and suggest the possibility that there should be more federal oversight of this process. Child support awards are determined at the state level, as is most of family law, and thus, it is perhaps not surprising that numerous aspects of child support vary widely from state to state (Pirog & Ziol-Guest, 2006), including whether or not an award is made, the amount of the award, the manner in which the award is determined, the method of payment (i.e., wage garnishment vs. private payments), and the enforcement methods. Because financial well-being is so critical for all involved, perhaps the federal government should step in to increase the uniformity involved in these aspects of the child support process. We recognize that there are some regional differences, such as cost of living variations, that justify some variation from region to region; federal guidelines could take these factors into account and ensure that each child has the best chance possible to receive the financial resources necessary to facilitate his or her development.

Third, laws should take into account the fluidity in adjustment over time by revisiting key legal decisions as the process unfolds. Currently, most divorce-related decisions are made at the time of the legal divorce settlement and no provisions are made for revisiting these decisions later when circumstances may change. Even if a cost-of-living factor is entered into the child support award, for example, there are usually no provisions for changing child support should one or both parents experience some major occupational change. Now, a parent must file a motion to modify the divorce decree to revisit the earlier arrangement. However, perhaps the fluid nature of divorce is sufficiently potent that it would be appropriate to build into divorce settlements some mechanism so that the decree will be reevaluated and possibly modified at some specified length of time after the divorce or if one or more of a designated set of special circumstances occurs. Thus, under this proposal, a parent would not need to take the initiative to change the divorce decree, but the court would be required to initiate a possible change at some predesignated time or event. For example, provisions could be made to revisit the custody arrangement when a young child enters school or again when he or she becomes an adolescent. Fluidity requires that the legal arrangements be modifiable as change unfolds.

Because of variability in outcomes and processes, policy makers should not assume that "one size fits all" solutions will work for everyone, such as preferences for joint custody or maternal custody. Rather, enough flexibility should be built into the laws so that the intricacies of each specific family's case can be taken into account. Laws have moved in that direction with the "best interests of the child" standard, which, by definition, takes into account an array of circumstances to determine what is best for each individual child. We support laws and guidelines that are flexible and sensitive to the wide variability in divorce-related experiences and adjustment and that have a keen appreciation for the likely (and even unlikely) changes that may occur over time.

〰 CONCLUSIONS

Our theoretical, empirical, clinical, and policy recommendations in this chapter have only touched the surface of the many possible avenues for future efforts. Our suggestions have been made with an eye toward illustrating how the DVFM can be employed to guide future scholarly and applied activities. In addition, we have deliberately chosen to restrict the scope of our recommendations to those that can be directly linked to our themes of variability and fluidity. We hope we have demonstrated the merits of looking beyond the average divorce. We also hope that engaged readers will find that some of the recommendations in this chapter, as well as other ideas described throughout the book, stimulate their own thinking and work in the extremely important divorce arena. Indeed, there is an ambitious scholarly and applied agenda requiring our attention, and we encourage professionals from many disciplines (e.g., family scientists, marriage and family therapists, psychologists, sociologists, nurses, communication scholars, and others) to take the lead in carrying the torch.

References

Ackerman, B., Kogos, J., Youngstrom, E., Schoff, K., & Izard, C. (1999). Family instability and the problem behaviors of children from economically disadvantaged families. *Developmental Psychology, 35,* 258–268.

Acock, A. C., & Demo, D. H. (1994). *Family diversity and well-being.* Thousand Oaks, CA: Sage.

Afifi, T. D. (2003). "Feeling caught" in stepfamilies: Managing boundary turbulence through appropriate privacy coordination rules. *Journal of Social and Personal Relationships, 20,* 729–756.

Afifi, T. D., McManus, T., Hutchinson, S., & Baker, B. (2007). Parental divorce disclosures, the factors that prompt them, and their impact on parents' and adolescents' well-being. *Communication Monographs, 74,* 78–103.

Ahrons, C. (2004). *We're still family.* New York: HarperCollins.

Albeck, S., & Kaydar, D. (2002). Divorced mothers: Their network of friends pre- and post-divorce. *Journal of Divorce and Remarriage, 36,* 111–138.

Aldous, J., & Ganey, R. F. (1999). Family life and the pursuit of happiness: The influence of gender and race. *Journal of Family Issues, 20,* 155–180.

Al-Krenawi, A., & Graham, J. R. (1998). Divorce among Muslim Arab women in Israel. *Journal of Divorce and Remarriage, 29,* 103–119.

Allen, K. R., Fine, M. A., & Demo, D. H. (2000). An overview of family diversity: Controversies, questions, and values. In D. H. Demo, K. R. Allen, & M. A. Fine (Eds.), *Handbook of family diversity* (pp. 1–14). New York: Oxford University Press.

Amato, P. R. (2000). The consequences of divorce for adults and children. *Journal of Marriage and the Family, 62,* 1269–1287.

Amato, P. R. (2001). Children of divorce in the 1990s: An update of the Amato and Keith (1991) meta-analysis. *Journal of Family Psychology, 15,* 355–370.

Amato, P. R. (2003). Reconciling divergent perspectives: Judith Wallerstein, quantitative family research, and children of divorce. *Family Relations, 52,* 332–339.

Amato, P. R. (2004). Tension between institutional and individual views of marriage. *Journal of Marriage and Family, 66,* 959–965.

Amato, P. R., & Afifi, T. D. (2006). Feeling caught between parents: Adult children's relations with parents and subjective well-being. *Journal of Marriage and Family, 68,* 222–235.

Amato, P. R., & Booth, A. (1996). A prospective study of parental divorce and parent–child relationships. *Journal of Marriage and the Family, 58,* 356–365.

Amato, P. R., & DeBoer, D. D. (2001). The transmission of marital instability across generations: Relationship skills or commitment to marriage? *Journal of Marriage and Family, 63,* 1038–1051.

Amato, P. R., & Hohmann-Marriott, B. (2007). A comparison of high- and low-distress marriages that end in divorce. *Journal of Marriage and Family, 69,* 621–638.

Amato, P. R., & Irving, S. (2006). Historical trends in divorce and dissolution in the United States. In M. A. Fine & J. H. Harvey (Eds.), *Handbook of divorce and relationship dissolution* (pp. 41–57). Mahwah, NJ: Lawrence Erlbaum.

Amato, P. R., & Keith, B. (1991). Consequences of parental divorce for the well-being of children: A meta-analysis. *Psychological Bulletin, 110,* 26–46.

Amato, P. R., Loomis, L. S., & Booth, A. (1995). Parental divorce, marital conflict, and offspring well-being during early adulthood. *Social Forces, 73,* 895–915.

Amato, P. R., & Previti, D. (2003). People's reasons for divorcing: Gender, social class, the life course, and adjustment. *Journal of Family Issues, 24,* 602–626.

Amato, P. R., & Rogers, S. J. (1997). A longitudinal study of marital problems and subsequent divorce. *Journal of Marriage and the Family, 59,* 612–624.

American Law Institute. (2002). *Principles of the law of family dissolution.* Philadelphia: LexisNexis.

Andersson, G. (2002). Dissolution of unions in Europe: A comparative overview. *Zeitschrift für Bevölkerungswissenschaft, 27,* 493–504. Also available as MPIDR Working Paper 2003-004. Max Planck Institute for Demographic Research, Rostock, Germany.

Andersson, G., Noack, T., Seierstad, A., & Weedon-Fekjaer, H. (2006). The demographics of same-sex marriages in Norway and Sweden. *Demography, 43,* 79–98.

Arditti, J. A. (1999). Rethinking relationships between divorced mothers and their children: Capitalizing on family strengths. *Family Relations, 48,* 109–119.

Arendell, T. (1995). *Fathers and divorce.* Thousand Oaks, CA: Sage.

Aseltine, R. H. (1996). Pathways linking parental divorce with adolescent depression. *Journal of Health and Social Behavior, 37,* 133–148.

Aseltine, R. H., & Kessler, R. C. (1993). Marital disruption and depression in a community sample. *Journal of Health and Social Behavior, 34,* 237–251.

Barber, B. L., & Demo, D. H. (2006). The kids are alright (at least, most of them): Links between divorce and dissolution and child well-being. In M. A. Fine & J. H. Harvey (Eds.), *Handbook of divorce and relationship dissolution* (pp. 289–311). Mahwah, NJ: Lawrence Erlbaum.

Baron, R. M., & Kenny, D. A. (1986). The moderator-mediator variable distinction in social psychological research: Conceptual, strategic and statistical considerations. *Journal of Personality and Social Psychology, 51,* 1173–1182.

Barrett, A. (2003). Race differences in the mental health effects of divorce: A reexamination incorporating temporal dimensions of the dissolution process. *Journal of Family Issues, 24,* 995–1019.

Bartell, D. S. (2006). Influence of parental divorce on romantic relationships in young adulthood: A cognitive-developmental perspective. In M. A. Fine & J. H. Harvey (Eds.), *Handbook of divorce and relationship dissolution* (pp. 339–360). Mahwah, NJ: Lawrence Erlbaum.

Battaglia, D. M., Richard, F. D., Datteri, D. L., & Lord, C. G. (1998). Breaking up is (relatively) easy to do: A script for the dissolution of close relationships. *Journal of Social and Personal Relationships, 15,* 829–845.

Baum, N. (2003). Divorce process variables and the co-parental relationship and parental role fulfillment of divorced parents. *Family Process, 42,* 117–131.

Bauserman, R. (2002). Child adjustment in joint-custody versus sole-custody arrangements: A meta-analytic review. *Journal of Family Psychology, 16,* 91–102.

Baxter, L. A. (1984). Trajectories of relationship disengagement. *Journal of Social and Personal Relationships, 1,* 29–48.

Bengtson, V. L., & Allen, K. R. (1993). The life course perspective applied to families over time. In P. G. Boss, W. J. Doherty, R. LaRossa, W. R. Schumm, & S. K. Steinmetz (Eds.), *Sourcebook of family theory and methods: A contextual approach* (pp. 469–499). New York: Plenum.

Bernard, J. (1972). *The future of marriage*. New Haven, CT: Yale University Press.

Bianchi, S. M., Robinson, J. P., & Milkie, M. A. (2006). *Changing rhythms of American family life*. New York: Russell Sage Foundation.

Bianchi, S. M., Subaiya, L., & Kahn, J. R. (1999). The gender gap in the economic well-being of nonresident fathers and custodial mothers. *Demography, 36*, 195–203.

Blaisure, K. R., & Geasler, M. J. (2006). Educational interventions for separating and divorcing parents and their children. In M. A. Fine & J. H. Harvey (Eds.), *Handbook of divorce and relationship dissolution* (pp. 575–602). Mahwah, NJ: Lawrence Erlbaum.

Block, J. H., Block, J., & Gjerde, P. F. (1986). The personality of children prior to divorce: A prospective study. *Child Development, 57*, 827–840.

Bodenmann, G., Charvoz, L., Bradbury, T. N., Bertoni, A., Iafrate, R., Guiliani, C., et al. (2007). The role of stress in divorce: A three-nation retrospective study. *Journal of Social and Personal Relationships, 24*, 707–728.

Bohannan, P. (1968). The six stations of divorce. In P. Bohannan (Ed.), *Divorce and after* (pp. 33–62). Garden City, NY: Doubleday.

Booth, A., & Amato, P. R. (1991). Divorce and psychological stress. *Journal of Health and Social Behavior, 32*, 396–407.

Booth, A., & Amato, P. R. (2001). Parental predivorce relations and offspring postdivorce well-being. *Journal of Marriage and Family, 63*, 197–212.

Bramlett, M. D., & Mosher, W. D. (2001). *First marriage dissolution, divorce, and remarriage: United States*. Advanced data from Vital and Health Statistics, No. 323. Washington, DC: U.S. Government Printing Office.

Bramlett, M., & Mosher, W. (2002). *Cohabitation, marriage, divorce, and remarriage in the United States* (Vital and Health Statistics, Series 23, No. 22). Washington, DC: U.S. Government Printing Office.

Braver, S. L., Shapiro, J. R., & Goodman, M. R. (2006). Consequences of divorce for parents. In M. A. Fine & J. H. Harvey (Eds.), *Handbook of divorce and relationship dissolution* (pp. 313–337). Mahwah, NJ: Lawrence Erlbaum.

Brody, G. H., Neubaum, E., & Forehand, R. (1988). Serial marriage: A heuristic analysis of an emerging family form. *Psychological Bulletin, 103*, 211–222.

Broman, C. L. (2002). Thinking of divorce, but staying married: The interplay of race and marital satisfaction. *Journal of Divorce and Remarriage, 37*(1/2), 151–161.

Bronfenbrenner, U. (1979). *The ecology of human development: Experiments by nature and design*. Cambridge, MA: Harvard University Press.

Bronfenbrenner, U. (1986). Ecology of the family as a context for human development: Research perspectives. *Developmental Psychology, 22*, 723–742.

Bronfenbrenner, U. (1989). Ecological systems theory. In R. Vasta (Ed.), *Annals of child development* (Vol. 6, pp. 187–249). Greenwich, CT: JAI.

Brown, S. L. (2006). Family structure transitions and adolescent well-being. *Demography, 43*, 447–461.

Bryant, C. M., & Conger, R. D. (1999). Marital success and domains of social support in long-term relationships: Does the influence of network members ever end? *Journal of Marriage and the Family, 61*, 437–450.

Buchanan, C. M., Maccoby, E. E., & Dornbusch, S. M. (1996). *Adolescents after divorce.* Cambridge, MA: Harvard University Press.

Buehler, C. (1987). Initiator status and the divorce transition. *Family Relations, 36,* 82–86.

Bumpass, L., & Lu, H. (2000). Trends in cohabitation and implications for children's family contexts. *Population Studies, 54,* 29–41.

Bumpass, L. L., & Raley, R. K. (1995). Redefining single-parent families: Cohabitation and changing family realities. *Demography, 32,* 97–109.

Burton, L. M., & Jayakody, R. (2001). Rethinking family structure and single parenthood: Implications for future studies of African American families and children. In A. Thornton (Ed.), *The well-being of children and families: Research and data needs* (pp. 127–153). Ann Arbor: University of Michigan Press.

Buunk, B. (1995). Sex, self-esteem, dependency, and extradyadic sexual experience as related to jealousy responses. *Journal of Social and Personal Relationships, 12,* 147–153.

Cano, A., & O'Leary, K. D. (2000). Infidelity and separations precipitate major depressive episodes and symptoms of nonspecific depression and anxiety. *Journal of Consulting and Clinical Psychology, 68,* 774–781.

Capaldi, D., Crosby, L., & Stoolmiller, M. (1996). Predicting the timing of first sexual intercourse for at-risk adolescent males. *Child Development, 67,* 344–359.

Capaldi, D. M., & Patterson, G. R. (1991). Relations of parental transitions to boys' adjustment problems. I. A linear hypothesis. II. Mothers at risk for transitions and unskilled parenting. *Developmental Psychology, 27,* 489–504.

Carlson, M. J. (2006). Family structure, father involvement, and adolescent behavioral outcomes. *Journal of Marriage and Family, 68,* 137–154.

Carlson, M. J., & Corcoran, M. E. (2001). Family structure and children's behavioral and cognitive outcomes. *Journal of Marriage and Family, 63,* 779–792.

Casper, L. M., & Bianchi, S. M. (2002). *Continuity and change in the American family.* Thousand Oaks, CA: Sage.

Cavanagh, S. E., Crissey, S. R., & Raley, R. K. (2008). Family structure history and adolescent romance. *Journal of Marriage and Family, 70,* 698–714.

Cavanagh, S. E., & Huston, A. C. (2006). Family instability and children's early problem behavior. *Social Forces, 85,* 551–581.

Cavanagh, S. E., & Huston, A. C. (2008). The timing of family instability and children's social development. *Journal of Marriage and Family, 70,* 1258–1270.

Centers for Disease Control. (2005). *Divorce rates by state: 1990, 1995, and 1999–2004.* Division of Vital Statistics, National Center for Health Statistics.

Chase-Lansdale, P. L., & Hetherington, E. M. (1990). The impact of divorce on life-span development: Short- and long-term effects. In D. L. Featherman & R. M. Lerner (Eds.), *Life-span development and behavior* (pp. 105–150). Hillsdale, NJ: Lawrence Erlbaum.

Cherlin, A. J. (1998). Marriage and marital dissolution among Black Americans. *Journal of Comparative Family Studies, 29,* 147–158.

Cherlin, A. J. (2004). The deinstitutionalization of American marriage. *Journal of Marriage and Family, 66,* 848–861.

Cherlin, A., Furstenberg, F., Chase-Lansdale, P., Kiernan, K., Robins, P., Morrison, D., & Teitler, J. (1991). Longitudinal studies of effects of divorce on children in Great Britain and the United States. *Science, 252,* 1386–1389.

Christensen, A., & Heavey, C. L. (1990). Gender and social structure in the demand/withdraw pattern of marital conflict. *Journal of Personality and Social Psychology, 59,* 73–81.

Clarke, S. C. (1995). *Advance report of final divorce statistics, 1989 and 1990* (Monthly vital statistics report, Vol. 43, No. 8, suppl.) Hyattsville, Maryland: National Center for Health Statistics.

Cohan, C. L., & Kleinbaum, S. (2002). Toward a greater understanding of the cohabitation effect: Premarital cohabitation and marital communication. *Journal of Marriage and Family, 64*, 180–192.

Cohen, O., & Savaya, R. (2003). Adjustment to divorce: A preliminary study among Muslim Arab citizens of Israel. *Family Process, 42*, 269–290.

Cohen, S., Klein, D. N., & O'Leary, K. D. (2007). The role of separation/divorce in relapse into and recovery from major depression. *Journal of Social and Personal Relationships, 24*, 855–873.

Colburn, K., Lin, P. L., & Moore, M. C. (1992). Gender and divorce experience. *Journal of Divorce and Remarriage, 17*, 87–108.

Coleman, M., Ganong, L., & Fine, M. A. (2000). Reinvestigating remarriage: Another decade of progress. *Journal of Marriage and the Family, 62*, 1288–1307.

Creswell, J. W. (1994). *Research design: Qualitative and quantitative approaches.* Thousand Oaks, CA: Sage.

Cretney, S. (2003). *Family law in the twentieth century: A history.* Oxford, UK: Oxford University Press.

Cummings, E. M., Goeke-Morey, M. C., & Papp, L. M. (2004). Everyday marital conflict and child aggression. *Journal of Abnormal Child Psychology, 32*, 191–202.

Cushman, D. P., & Cahn, D. D. (1986). A study of communicative realignment between parents and children following the parent's decision to seek a divorce. *Communication Research Reports, 3*, 80–85.

Davies, L., Avison, W. R., & McAlpine, D. D. (1997). Significant life experiences and depression among single and married mothers. *Journal of Marriage and the Family, 59*, 294–308.

DeMaris, A. (2000). Till discord do us part: The role of physical and verbal conflict in union disruption. *Journal of Marriage and the Family, 62*, 683–692.

Demo, D. H., & Acock, A. C. (1996a). Family structure, family process, and adolescent well-being. *Journal of Research on Adolescence, 6*, 457–488.

Demo, D. H., & Acock, A. C. (1996b). Motherhood, marriage, and remarriage: The effects of family structure and family relationships on mothers' well-being. *Journal of Family Issues, 17*, 388–407.

Demo, D. H., Aquilino, W. S., & Fine, M. A. (2005). Family composition and family transitions. In V. Bengsten, A. Acock, K. Allen, P. Dilworth-Anderson, & D. Klein (Eds.), *Sourcebook of family theory and research* (pp. 119–134). Thousand Oaks, CA: Sage.

Demo, D. H., & Cox, M. J. (2000). Families with young children: A review of research in the 1990s. *Journal of Marriage and the Family, 62*, 876–895.

Doherty, W. J., & Needle, R. H. (1991). Psychological adjustment and substance abuse among adolescents before and after a parental divorce. *Child Development, 62*, 328–337.

Dohrenwend, B. S., & Dohrenwend, B. (1974). *Stressful life events: Their nature and effects.* New York: Wiley.

Ducibella, J. S. (1995). Consideration of the impact of how children are informed of their parents' divorce decision: A review of the literature. *Journal of Divorce and Remarriage, 24*, 121–141.

Duck, S. W. (1982). A topography of relationship disengagement and dissolution. In S. W. Duck (Ed.), *Personal relationships 4: Dissolving personal relationships* (pp. 1–30). London: Academic Press.

Duck, S. W. (2005). How do you tell some one you're letting go? A new model of relationship break up. *The Psychologist, 18,* 210–213.

Dunifon, R., & Kowaleski-Jones, L. (2002). Who's in the house? Race differences in cohabitation, single parenthood, and child development. *Child Development, 73,* 1249–1264.

Duran-Aydintug, C. (1995). Former spouses exiting role-identities. *Journal of Divorce and Remarriage, 24,* 23–39.

Elder, G. H., Jr. (1977). Family history and the life course. *Journal of Family History, 2,* 279–304.

Elder, G. H., Jr. (1991). Life course. In E. F. Borgotta & M. L. Borgotta (Eds.), *The encyclopedia of sociology* (pp. 281–311). New York: MacMillan.

Elder, G. H., Jr. (1994). Time, human agency, and social change. *Social Psychology Quarterly, 57,* 4–15.

Elder, G. H., Jr. (1998). The life course as developmental theory. *Child Development, 69,* 1–12.

Eldridge, K. A., & Christensen, A. (2002). Demand-withdraw communication during couple conflict: A review and analysis. In P. Noller & J. A Feeney (Eds.), *Understanding marriage* (pp. 289–322). Cambridge, UK: Cambridge University Press.

Ellis, B. J., Bates, J. E., Dodge, K. A., Fergusson, D. M., Horwood, L. J., Pettit, G. S., & Woodward, L. (2003). Does father absence place daughters at special risk for early sexual-activity and teenage pregnancy? *Child Development, 74,* 801–821.

Emery, R. E. (1994). *Renegotiating family relationships.* New York: Guilford Press.

Emery, R. E. (1999). *Marriage, divorce, and children's adjustment.* Thousand Oaks, CA: Sage.

Emery, R. E., & Forehand, R. (1994). Parental divorce and children's well-being: A focus on resilience. In R. J. Haggerty, L. R. Sherrod, N. Garmezy, & M. Rutter (Eds.), *Stress, risk, and resilience in children and adolescents: Processes, mechanisms, and interactions* (pp. 65–99). New York: Cambridge University Press.

Emery, R. E., Waldron, M., Kitzmann, K. M., & Aaron, J. (1999). Delinquent behavior, future divorce or nonmarital childbearing, and externalizing behavior among offspring: A 14 year prospective study. *Journal of Family Psychology, 13,* 568–579.

Erickson, R. J. (2005). Why emotion work matters: Sex, gender, and the division of household labor. *Journal of Marriage and Family, 67,* 337–351.

Faison, S. (1994, August 22). Divorce in modern China. *New York Times.* Retrieved from http://acc6.its.brooklyn.cuny.edu/~phalsall/texts/chinwomn.html

Felson, R. B. (2002). *Violence and gender reexamined.* Washington, DC: American Psychological Association.

Femlee, D. H. (1995). Fatal attractions: Affection and disaffection in intimate relationships. *Journal of Social and Personal Relationships, 12,* 295–311.

Fine, M. A. (2000). Divorce and single parenting. In C. Hendrick & S. S. Hendrick (Eds.), *Sourcebook of close relationships* (pp. 139–152). Thousand Oaks, CA: Sage.

Fine, M. A., Coleman, M., Gable, S., Ganong, L. H., Ispa, J., Morrison, J., & Thornburg, K. R. (1999). Research-based parenting education for divorcing parents: A university-community collaboration. In T. R. Chibocos & R. M. Lerner (Eds.), *Serving children and families through community-university partnerships: Success stories* (pp. 249–256). Norwell, MA: Kluwer.

Fine, M. A., & Fine, D. R. (1994). An examination and evaluation of recent changes in divorce laws in five Western countries: The critical role of values. *Journal of Marriage and the Family, 56,* 249–263.

Fine, M. A., & Harvey, J. H. (2006a). Divorce and relationship dissolution in the 21st century. In M. A. Fine & J. H. Harvey (Eds.), *Handbook of divorce and relationship dissolution* (pp. 3–11). Mahwah, NJ: Lawrence Erlbaum.

Fine, M. A., & Harvey, J. H. (2006b). *Handbook of divorce and relationship dissolution.* Mahwah, NJ: Lawrence Erlbaum.

Fomby, P., & Cherlin, A. J. (2007). Family instability and child well-being. *American Sociological Review, 72,* 181–204.

Foster, E. M., & Kalil, A. (2007). Living arrangements and children's development in low-income White, Black, and Latino families. *Child Development, 78,* 1657–1674.

Furstenberg, F. F., & Teitler, J. O. (1994). Reconsidering the effects of marital disruption: What happens to children of divorce in early adulthood? *Journal of Family Issues, 15,* 173–190.

Gager, C. T., & Sanchez, L. (2003). Two as one? Couples' perceptions of time spent together, marital quality, and the risk of divorce. *Journal of Family Issues, 24,* 21–50.

Gähler, M. (1998). *Life after divorce: Economic, social, and psychological well-being among Swedish adults and children following family dissolution.* Published doctoral dissertation, Stockholm University, Swedish Institute for Social Research.

Ganong, L., Coleman, M., & Hans, J. (2006). Divorce as prelude to stepfamily living and the consequences of redivorce. In M. A. Fine & J. H. Harvey (Eds.), *Handbook of divorce and relationship dissolution* (pp. 409–434). Mahwah, NJ: Lawrence Erlbaum.

Gartrell, N., Banks, A., Reed, N., Hamilton, J., Rodas, C., & Deck, A. (2000). The national lesbian family study III: Interviews with mothers of 5 year olds. *American Journal of Orthopsychiatry, 70,* 542–548.

George, A. L., & Bennett, A. (2005). *Case studies and theory development in the social sciences.* Boston: MIT Press.

Gigy, L., & Kelly, J. B. (1992). Reasons for divorce: Perspectives of divorcing men and women. *Journal of Divorce and Remarriage, 18,* 169–187.

Glenn, N. D. (1998). The course of marital success and failure in five American 10-year marriage cohorts. *Journal of Marriage and the Family, 60,* 569–576.

Goldstein, J. R., & Kenney, C. T. (2001). Marriage delayed or marriage forgone? New cohort forecasts of first marriage for U.S. women. *American Sociological Review, 66,* 506–519.

Gottman, J. (1993). A theory of marital dissolution and stability. *Journal of Family Psychology, 7,* 57–75.

Gottman, J. (1994). *What predicts divorce.* Hillsdale, NJ: Lawrence Erlbaum.

Gottman, J. M., Coan, C., Carrere, S., & Swanson, C. (1998). Predicting marital happiness and stability from newlywed couples. *Journal of Marriage and the Family, 60,* 5–22.

Gottman, J. M., & Levenson, R. W. (2000). The timing of divorce: Predicting when a couple will divorce over a 14-year period. *Journal of Marriage and the Family, 62,* 737–745.

Gottman, J. M., & Notarius, C. I. (2000). Decade review: Observing marital interaction. *Journal of Marriage and the Family, 62,* 927–947.

Gregory, J. D., Swisher, P. N., & Wolf, S. L. (2001). *Understanding family law* (2nd ed.). New York: Matthew Bender.

Hagestad, G. O., & Smyer, M. A. (1982). Dissolving long-term relationships: Patterns of divorcing in middle age. *Personal relationships 4: Dissolving personal relationships* (pp. 155–187). London: Academic Press.

Hall, J. H., & Fincham, F. D. (2006). Relationship dissolution following infidelity. In M. A. Fine & J. H. Harvey (Eds.), *Handbook of divorce and relationship dissolution* (pp. 153–168). Mahwah, NJ: Lawrence Erlbaum.

Halpern-Meekin, S., & Tach, L. (2008). Heterogeneity in two-parent families and adolescent well-being. *Journal of Marriage and Family, 70,* 435–451.

Hanson, T. L., McLanahan, S., & Thomson, E. (1998). Windows on divorce: Before and after. *Social Science Research, 27,* 329–349.

Hareven, T. K. (1987). Historical analysis of the family. In M. B. Sussman & S. K. Steinmetz (Eds.), *Handbook of marriage and the family* (pp. 37–57). New York: Plenum.

Harvey, J. H., & Fine, M. A. (2004). *Children of divorce: Stories of loss and growth.* Mahwah, NJ: Lawrence Erlbaum.

Harvey, J. H., & Fine, M. A. (2006). Social construction of accounts in the process of relationship termination. In M. A. Fine & J. H. Harvey (Eds.), *Handbook of divorce and relationship dissolution* (pp. 189–199). Mahwah, NJ: Lawrence Erlbaum.

Harvey, J. H., Weber, A. L., & Orbuch, T. L. (1990). *Interpersonal accounts.* Oxford, England: Blackwell.

Hawkins, A. J., Nock, S. L., Wilson, J. C., Sanchez, L., & Wright, J. D. (2002). Attitudes about covenant marriage and divorce: Policy implications from a three-state comparison. *Family Relations, 51,* 166–175.

Hays, S. (1996). *The cultural contradictions of motherhood.* New Haven, CT: Yale University Press.

Heard, H. E. (2007). Fathers, mothers, and family structure: Family trajectories, parent gender, and adolescent schooling. *Journal of Marriage and Family, 69,* 435–450.

Heaton, T. B., & Albrecht, S. L. (1991). Stable unhappy marriages. *Journal of Marriage and the Family, 53,* 747–758.

Heavey, C. L., Christensen, A., & Malamuth, N. M. (1995). The longitudinal impact of demand and withdrawal during marital conflict. *Journal of Consulting and Clinical Psychology, 63,* 797–801.

Helms, H. M., & Demo, D. H. (2005). Everyday hassles and family stress. In P. C. McKenry & S. J. Price (Eds.), *Families and change: Coping with stressful events and transitions* (pp. 355–378). Thousand Oaks, CA: Sage.

Hetherington, E. M. (1999). Should we stay together for the sake of the children? In E. M. Hetherington (Ed.), *Coping with divorce, single parenting, and remarriage* (pp. 93–116). Mahwah, NJ: Lawrence Erlbaum.

Hetherington, E. M. (2003). Intimate pathways: Changing patterns in close personal relationships across time. *Family Relations, 52,* 318–331.

Hetherington, E. M., Bridges, M., & Insabella, G. M. (1998). What matters? What does not? Five perspectives on the association between marital transitions and children's adjustment. *American Psychologist, 53,* 167–184.

Hetherington, E. M., & Kelly, J. (2002). *For better or for worse: Divorce reconsidered.* New York: W. W. Norton.

Hewitt, B., Western, M., & Baxter, J. (2006). Who decides? The social characteristics of who initiates marital separation. *Journal of Marriage and Family, 68,* 1165–1177.

Heyman, R. E., & Smith Slep, A. M. (2001). The hazards of predicting divorce without crossvalidation. *Journal of Marriage and Family, 63,* 473–479.

Hochschild, A. (with Machung, A.). (2003). *The second shift: Working parents and the revolution at home* (Rev. ed.). New York: Viking/Penguin.

Hoffmann, J. P. (2002). The community context of family structure and adolescent drug use. *Journal of Marriage and Family, 64,* 314–330.

Hopper, J. (1993). The rhetoric of motives in divorce. *Journal of Marriage and the Family, 55,* 801–813.

Hopper, J. (2001). The symbolic origins of conflict in divorce. *Journal of Marriage and Family, 63,* 430–445.

Horwitz, A. V., White, H. R., & Howell-White, S. (1996). The use of multiple outcomes in stress research: A case study of gender differences in responses to marital dissolution. *Journal of Health and Social Behavior, 37,* 278–291.

Huang, P. C. C. (2007). Whither Chinese law. *Modern China, 33*(2), 163–194.

Hurley, D. (2005, April 19). Divorce rate: It's not as high as you think. *New York Times.* Retrieved from http://www.divorcereform.org/nyt05.html

Huston, T. L., Caughlin, J. P., Houts, R. M., Smith, S. E., & George, L. J. (2001). The connubial crucible: Newlywed years as predictors of marital delight, distress, and divorce. *Journal of Personality and Social Psychology, 80,* 237–252.

Huston, T. L., & Houts, R. M. (1998). The psychological infrastructure of courtship and marriage: The role of personality and compatibility in romantic relationships. In T. N. Bradbury (Ed.), *The developmental course of marital dysfunction* (pp. 114–151). Cambridge, UK: Cambridge University Press.

Inglehart, R. (1997). *Modernization and postmodernization: Cultural, economic, and political change in 43 societies.* Princeton, NJ: Princeton University Press.

Jacobson, N., & Gottman, J. (1998). *When men batter women: New insights into enduring abusive relationships.* New York: Simon and Schuster.

Jacobson, N. S., Gottman, J. M., Gortner, E., Burns, S., & Shortt, J. W. (1996). Psychological factors in the longitudinal course of battering: When do couples split up? When does abuse decrease? *Violence and Victims, 11,* 371–392.

Jacquet, S. E., & Surra, C. A. (2001). Parental divorce and premarital couples: Commitment and other relationship characteristics. *Journal of Marriage and Family, 63,* 627–638.

Jekielek, S. M. (1998). Parental conflict, marital disruption and children's emotional well-being. *Social Forces, 76,* 905–935.

Johnson, D. R., & Wu, J. (2002). An empirical test of crisis, social selection, and role explanations of the relationship between marital disruption and psychological distress: A pooled time-series analysis of four-wave panel data. *Journal of Marriage and Family, 64,* 211–224.

Johnson, M. P., & Ferraro, K. J. (2000). Research on domestic violence in the 1990s: Making distinctions. *Journal of Marriage and the Family, 62,* 948–963.

Kalmijn, M., & Monden, C. W. S. (2006). Are the negative effects of divorce on well-being dependent on marital quality? *Journal of Marriage and Family, 68,* 1197–1213.

Karney, B. R., & Bradbury, T. (1995). The longitudinal course of marital quality and stability: A review of theory, method, and research. *Psychological Bulletin, 118,* 3–34.

Kayser, K., & Rao, S. S. (2006). Process of disaffection in relationship breakdown. In M. A. Fine & J. H. Harvey (Eds.), *Handbook of divorce and relationship dissolution* (pp. 201–221). Mahwah, NJ: Lawrence Erlbaum.

Kellas, J. K., & Manusov, V. (2003). What's in a story? The relationship between narrative completeness and adjustment to relationship dissolution. *Journal of Social and Personal Relationships, 20,* 285–307.

Kelly, J. B., & Emery, R. E. (2003). Children's adjustment following divorce: Risk and resilience perspectives. *Family Relations, 52,* 352–362.

Kent, D., & Peplar, D. (2003). The aggressive child as agent in coercive family processes. In L. Kuczynski (Ed.), *Handbook of dynamics in parent–child relations* (pp. 131–144). Thousand Oaks, CA: Sage.

Kim, H. K., & McKenry, P. C. (2002). The relationship between marriage and psychological well-being: A longitudinal analysis. *Journal of Family Issues, 23,* 885–911.

King, V. (1994). Nonresident father involvement and child well-being: Can dads make a difference? *Journal of Family Issues, 15,* 78–96.

King, V., Harris, K. H., & Heard, H. E. (2004). Racial and ethnic diversity in nonresident father involvement. *Journal of Marriage and Family, 66,* 1–21.

Kitson, G. C. (1992). *Portrait of divorce: Adjustment to marital breakdown.* New York: Guilford Press.

Klinetob, N. A., & Smith, D. A. (1996). Demand-withdraw communication in marital interaction: Tests of interpersonal contingency and gender role hypotheses. *Journal of Marriage and the Family, 58,* 945–957.

Kluwer, E. S., Heesink, J. A. M., & van de Vliert, E. (1997). The marital dynamics of conflict over the division of labor. *Journal of Marriage and the Family, 59,* 635–653.

Knoester, C., & Booth, A. (2000). Barriers to divorce: When are they effective? When are they not? *Journal of Family Issues, 21,* 78–99.

Knox, D., & Corte, U. (2007). "Work it out/see a counselor": Advice from spouses in the separation process. *Journal of Divorce and Remarriage, 48,* 79–90.

Koerner, S. S., Jacobs, S. L., & Raymond, M. (2002). Mother-to-daughter disclosure after divorce: Are there costs and benefits? *Journal of Child and Family Studies, 11,* 469–483.

Krause, H. D., & Meyer, D. D. (2003). *Family law: In a nutshell* (4th ed.). Minneapolis, MN: West.

Kreider, R. M. (2007). *Living arrangements of children: 2004.* Current Population Reports, P70-114. Washington, DC: U.S. Census Bureau.

Kreider, R. M., & Fields, J. M. (2002). *Number, timing, and duration of marriages and divorces: 1996.* Current Population Reports, P70-80. Washington, DC: U.S. Census Bureau.

Kunz, J. (2001). Parental divorce and children's interpersonal relationships: A meta-analysis. *Journal of Divorce and Remarriage, 34,* 19–47.

Kunz, J., & Kunz, P. R. (1995). Social support during the process of divorce: It does make a difference. *Journal of Divorce and Remarriage, 24,* 111–119.

Kurdek, L. A. (1990). Divorce history and self-reported psychological distress in husbands and wives. *Journal of Marriage and the Family, 52,* 701–708.

Kurdek, L. A. (1992). Relationship stability and relationship satisfaction in cohabiting gay and lesbian couples: A prospective longitudinal test of the contextual and interdependence models. *Journal of Social and Personal Relationships, 9,* 125–142.

Kurdek, L. A. (1995). Predicting change in marital satisfaction from husbands' and wives' conflict resolution styles. *Journal of Marriage and the Family, 57,* 153–164.

Kurdek, L. A. (1998). Developmental changes in marital satisfaction: A 6-year prospective longitudinal study of newlywed couples. In T. N. Bradbury (Ed.), *The developmental course of marital dysfunction* (pp. 180–204). Cambridge, UK: Cambridge University Press.

Kurdek, L. A. (2002). Predicting the timing of separation and marital satisfaction: An eight-year prospective longitudinal study. *Journal of Marriage and Family, 64,* 163–179.

Kurdek, L. A., & Fine, M. A. (1994). Family acceptance and family control as predictors of adjustment problems in young adolescents: Linear, curvilinear, or interactive effects? *Child Development, 65,* 1137–1146.

Kurdek, L. A., Fine, M. A., & Sinclair, R. J. (1994). The relation between parenting transitions and adjustment in young adolescents: A multi-sample investigation. *Journal of Early Adolescence, 14,* 412–432.

Kurdek, L. A., Fine, M. A., & Sinclair, R. J. (1995). School adjustment in sixth graders: Parenting transitions, family climate, and peer norm effects. *Child Development, 66,* 430–445.

Lansford, J. E., Malone, D., Castellino, D. R., Dodge, K., Petit, G., & Bates, J. (2006). Trajectories of internalizing, externalizing, and grades for children who have and have not experienced their parents' divorce or separation. *Journal of Family Psychology, 20,* 292–301.

Lawrence, E., & Bradbury, T. N. (2001). Physical aggression and marital dysfunction: A longitudinal analysis. *Journal of Family Psychology, 15,* 135–154.

Lawrence, E., Ro, E., Barry, R., & Bunde, M. (2006). Mechanisms of distress and dissolution in physically aggressive romantic relationships. In M. A. Fine & J. H. Harvey (Eds.), *Handbook of divorce and relationship dissolution* (pp. 263–286). Mahwah, NJ: Lawrence Erlbaum.

Lawson, E. J., & Thompson, A. (1999). *Black men and divorce.* Thousand Oaks, CA: Sage.

Leary, M. R., Springer, C., Negel, L., Ansell, E., & Evans, K. (1998). The causes, phenomenology, and consequences of hurt feelings. *Journal of Personality and Social Psychology, 74,* 1225–1237.

Lee, L. (1984). Sequences in separation: A framework for investigating the endings of personal (romantic) relationships. *Journal of Social and Personal Relationships, 1,* 49–74.

Lee, M. (2002). A model of children's postdivorce behavioral adjustment in maternal and dual-residence arrangements. *Journal of Family Issues, 23,* 672–697.

Leonard, K. E., & Roberts, L. J. (1998). Marital aggression, quality, and stability in the first year of marriage: Findings from the Buffalo newlywed study. In T. N. Bradbury (Ed.), *The developmental course of marital dysfunction* (pp. 44–73). New York: Cambridge University Press.

Levinger, G. (1979). A social exchange view of the dissolution of pair relationship. In R. L. Burgess & T. L. Huston (Eds.), *Social exchange: Advances in theory and research* (pp. 169–193). New York: Academic Press.

Lindahl, K., Clements, M., & Markman, H. (1998). The development of marriage: A 9-year perspective. In T. N. Bradbury (Ed.), *The developmental course of marital dysfunction* (pp. 205–236). Cambridge, UK: Cambridge University Press.

Lorenz, F. O., Simons, R. L., Conger, R. D., Elder, G. H., Johnson, C., & Chao, W. (1997). Married and recently divorced mothers' stressful events and distress: Tracing change across time. *Journal of Marriage and the Family, 59,* 219–232.

Maccoby, E. E., & Mnookin, R. H. (1992). *Dividing the child: Social and legal dilemmas of custody.* Cambridge, MA: Harvard University Press.

Mahoney, M. (2006). The law of divorce and relationship dissolution. In M. A. Fine & J. H. Harvey (Eds.), *Handbook of divorce and relationship dissolution* (pp. 533–552). Mahwah, NJ: Lawrence Erlbaum.

Manning, W. D., & Smock, P. J. (2000). Swapping families: Serial parenting and economic consequences for children. *Journal of Marriage and the Family, 62,* 111–122.

Manning, W. D., Smock, P. J., & Majumdar, D. (2004). The relative stability of cohabiting and marital unions for children. *Population Research and Policy Review, 23,* 135–159.

Marks, N. F. (1996). Flying solo at midlife: Gender, marital status, and psychological well-being. *Journal of Marriage and the Family, 58,* 917–932.

Martinez, C. R. J., & Forgatch, M. S. (2002). Adjusting to change: Linking family structure transitions with parenting and boys' adjustment. *Journal of Family Psychology, 16,* 107–117.

Mason, M. A. (2000). *The custody wars.* New York: Basic Books.

Mason, M. A., Fine, M. A., & Carnochan, S. (2001). Family law in the new millenium: For whose families? *Journal of Family Issues, 22,* 859–881.

Mastekaasa, A. (1994). Psychological well-being and marital dissolution: Selection effects. *Journal of Family Issues, 15,* 208–228.

Mastekaasa, A. (1997). Marital dissolution as a stressor: Some evidence on psychological, physical, and behavioral changes during the preseparation period. *Journal of Divorce and Remarriage, 26,* 155–183.

Masuda, M. (2006). Perspectives on premarital dissolution relationships: Account-making of friendships between former romantic partners. In M. A. Fine & J. H. Harvey (Eds.), *Handbook of divorce and relationship dissolution* (pp. 113–132). Mahwah, NJ: Lawrence Erlbaum.

Matthews, L. S., Wickrama, K. A. S., & Conger, R. D. (1996). Predicting marital instability from spouse and observer reports of marital interaction. *Journal of Marriage and the Family, 58,* 641–655.

McLanahan, S. S., & Sandefur, G. (1994). *Growing up with a single parent: What hurts, what helps.* Cambridge, MA: Harvard University Press.

McManus, P. A., & DiPrete, T. A. (2001). Losers and winners: The financial consequences of separation and divorce for men. *American Sociological Review, 66,* 246–268.

Miles, M. B., & Huberman, A. M. (1994). *Qualitative data analysis* (2nd ed.). Thousand Oaks, CA: Sage.

Mills, C. W. (1959). *The sociological imagination.* London: Oxford University Press.

Mnookin, R. H., & Kornhauser, L. (1979). Bargaining in the shadow of the law: The case of divorce. *Yale Law Journal, 88,* 950–997.

Morgan, L. W. (1996). *Child support guidelines: Interpretation and application.* New York: Aspen Law and Business (Suppl., 2001).

Morrison, D. R., & Cherlin, A. J. (1995). The divorce process and young children's well-being: A prospective analysis. *Journal of Marriage and the Family, 57,* 800–812.

Moxnes, K. (2003). Risk factors in divorce: Perceptions by the children involved. *Childhood, 10*(2), 131–146.

Neff, J. A., & Schluter, T. D. (1993). Marital status and depressive symptoms: The role of race/ethnicity and sex. *Journal of Divorce and Remarriage, 20,* 137–160.

Nelson, T. J. (2004). Low-income fathers. *Annual Review of Sociology, 30,* 427–451.

Oldehinkel, A. J., Ormel, J., Veenstra, R., DeWinter, A. F., & Verhulst, F. C. (2008). Parental divorce and offspring depressive symptoms: Dutch developmental trends during early adolescence. *Journal of Marriage and Family, 70,* 284–293.

Orbuch, T. L., & Brown, E. (2006). Divorce in the context of being African American. In M. A. Fine & J. H. Harvey (Eds.), *Handbook of divorce and relationship dissolution* (pp. 481–498). Mahwah, NJ: Lawrence Erlbaum.

Orbuch, T. L., Veroff, J., Hassan, H., & Horrocks, J. (2002). Who will divorce: A 14-year longitudinal study of black couples and white couples. *Journal of Social and Personal Relationships, 19,* 179–202.

Osborne, C., Manning, W. D., & Smock, P. J. (2007). Married and cohabiting parents' relationship stability: A focus on race and ethnicity. *Journal of Marriage and Family, 69,* 1345–1366.

Osborne, C., & McLanahan, S. (2007). Partnership instability and child well-being. *Journal of Marriage and Family, 69,* 1065–1083.

Osmond, M. W., & Thorne, B. (1993). Feminist theories: The social construction of gender in families and society. In P. G. Boss, W. J. Doherty, R. LaRossa, W. R. Schumm, & S. K. Steinmetz (Eds.), *Sourcebook of family theory and methods: A contextual approach* (pp. 591–623). New York: Plenum.

Pennebaker, J., Zech, E., & Rimé, B. (2001). Disclosing and sharing emotion: Psychological, social, and health consequences. In M. Stroebe, R. O. Hansson, W. Stroebe, & H. Schut (Eds.), *Handbook of bereavement research: Consequences, coping, and care* (pp. 517–543). Washington, DC: American Psychological Association.

Pett, M. A., Wampold, B. E., Turner, C. W., & Vaughan-Cole, B. (1999). Paths of influence of divorce on preschool children's psychosocial adjustment. *Journal of Family Psychology, 13*, 145–164.

Phillips, R. (1991). *Untying the knot: A brief history of divorce*. Cambridge, UK: Cambridge University Press.

Pirog, M. A., & Ziol-Guest, M. (2006). Child support enforcement: Programs and policies, impacts and questions. *Journal of Policy Analysis and Management, 25*, 943–990.

Pirog-Good, M. A. (1993). Child support guidelines and the economic well-being of children in the United States. *Family Relations, 42*, 453–462.

Pleck, J. H. (1997). Paternal involvement: Levels, sources, and consequences. In E. M. Lamb (Ed.), *The role of the father in child development* (3rd ed., pp. 66–103). New York: Wiley.

Pong, S., & Ju, D. (2000). The effects of change in family structure and income on dropping out of middle and high school. *Journal of Family Issues, 21*, 147–169.

Popenoe, D. (1993). American family decline, 1960–1990: A review and appraisal. *Journal of Marriage and the Family, 55*, 527–542.

Popenoe, D. (1996). *Life without father*. New York: Free Press.

Raley, R. K., & Wildsmith, E. (2004). Cohabitation and children's family instability. *Journal of Marriage and Family, 66*, 210–219.

Reifman, A., Villa, L., Amans, J., Rethinam, V., & Telesca, T. (2001). Children of divorce in the 1990s: A meta-analysis. *Journal of Divorce and Remarriage, 36*, 27–36.

Riessman, C. K. (1990). *Divorce talk: Women and men make sense of personal relationships*. London: Rutgers University Press.

Rimm-Kaufman, S. E., & Pianta, R. C. (2000). An ecological perspective on the transition to kindergarten: A theoretical framework to guide empirical research. *Journal of Applied Developmental Psychology, 21*, 491–511.

Roberts, L. J. (2000). Fire and ice in marital communication: Hostile and distancing behaviors as predictors of marital distress. *Journal of Marriage and the Family, 62*, 693–707.

Rodgers, K. B., & Rose, H. A. (2002). Risk and resiliency factors among adolescents who experience marital transitions. *Journal of Marriage and Family, 64*, 1024–1037.

Rodrigues, A. E., Hall, J. H., & Fincham, F. D. (2006). What predicts divorce and relationship dissolution. In M. A. Fine & J. H. Harvey (Eds.), *Handbook of divorce and relationship dissolution* (pp. 85–112). Mahwah, NJ: Lawrence Erlbaum.

Rogge, R. D., & Bradbury, T. N. (1999). Till violence does us part: The differing roles of communication and aggression in predicting adverse marital outcomes. *Journal of Consulting and Clinical Psychology, 67*, 340–351.

Rokach, R., Cohen, O., & Dreman, S. (2004). Who pulls the trigger? Who initiates divorce among over 45-year-olds. *Journal of Divorce and Remarriage, 42*, 61–83.

Rollie, S. S. (2006). Nonresidential parent–child relationships: Overcoming the challenges of absence. In S. Duck, D. C. Kirkpatrick, & M. Foley (Eds.), *Difficult relationships* (pp. 181–201). Mahwah, NJ: Lawrence Erlbaum.

Rollie, S. S., & Duck, S. (2006). Divorce and dissolution of romantic relationships: Stage models and their limitations. In M. A. Fine & J. H. Harvey (Eds.), *Handbook of divorce and relationship dissolution* (pp. 223–240). Mahwah, NJ: Lawrence Erlbaum.

Ross, C. E. (1995). Reconceptualizing marital status as a continuum of social attachment. *Journal of Marriage and the Family, 57,* 129–140.

Rubin, K. H., & Burgess, K. B. (2002). Parents of aggressive and withdrawn children. In M. H. Bornstein (Ed.), *Handbook of parenting: Vol. 1. Children and parenting* (2nd ed., pp. 383–418). Mahwah, NJ: Lawrence Erlbaum.

Rusbult, C. E., & Buunk, B. P. (1993). Commitment processes in close relationships: An interdependence analysis. *Journal of Social and Personal Relationships, 10,* 175–204.

Rutter, M. (1994). Family discord and conduct disorder: Cause, consequence, or correlate? *Journal of Family Psychology, 8,* 170–186.

Sakraida, T. (2005). Divorce transition differences of midlife women. *Issues in Mental Health Nursing, 26,* 225–249.

Sanchez, L., & Gager, C. T. (2000). Hard living, perceived entitlement to a great marriage, and marital dissolution. *Journal of Marriage and the Family, 62,* 708–722.

Sayer, L. C. (2006). Economic aspects of divorce and relationship dissolution. In M. A. Fine & J. H. Harvey (Eds.), *Handbook of divorce and relationship dissolution* (pp. 385–406). Mahwah, NJ: Lawrence Erlbaum.

Scott, M. E., Booth, A., King, V., & Johnson, D. R. (2007). Postdivorce father-adolescent closeness. *Journal of Marriage and Family, 69,* 1194–1209.

Serido, J., Almeida, D. M., & Wethington, E. (2004). Chronic stressors and daily hassles: Unique and interactive relationships with psychological distress. *Journal of Health and Social Behavior, 45,* 17–33.

Shapiro, A. D. (1996). Explaining psychological distress in a sample of remarried and divorced persons: The influence of economic distress. *Journal of Family Issues, 17,* 186–203.

Shaw, D. S., Emery, R. E., & Tuer, M. D. (1993). Parental functioning and children's adjustment in families of divorce: A prospective study. *Journal of Abnormal Child Psychology, 21,* 119–134.

Shehan, C. L., Berardo, F. M., Owens, E., & Berardo, D. H. (2002). Alimony: An anomaly in family social science. *Family Relations, 51,* 308–316.

Simon, R. W., & Marcussen, K. (1999). Marital transitions, marital beliefs, and mental health. *Journal of Health and Social Behavior, 40,* 111–125.

Simons, R. L., & Associates. (1996). *Understanding differences between divorced and intact families.* Thousand Oaks, CA: Sage.

Smerglia, E. L., Miller, N. B., & Kort-Butler, L. (1999). The impact of social support on women's adjustment to divorce: A literature review and analysis. *Journal of Divorce and Remarriage, 23,* 63–89.

Smock, P. J. (1993). The economic costs of marital disruption for young women over the past two decades. *Demography, 30,* 353–371.

Smock, P. J., Manning, W. D., & Gupta, S. (1999). The effect of marriage and divorce on women's economic well-being. *American Sociological Review, 64,* 794–812.

South, S. J., Trent, K., & Shen, Y. (2001). Changing partners: Toward a macrostructural-opportunity theory of marital dissolution. *Journal of Marriage and Family, 63,* 743–754.

Sprecher, S., Felmlee, D., Schmeeckle, M., & Shu, X. (2006). No breakup occurs on an island: Social networks and relationship dissolution. In M. Fine & J. Harvey (Eds.), *Handbook of divorce and relationship dissolution* (pp. 457–478). Mahwah, NJ: Lawrence Erlbaum.

Stacey, J. (1993). Good riddance to "The family": A response to David Popenoe. *Journal of Marriage and the Family, 55,* 545–547.

Stanley, S. M., Bradbury, T. N., & Markman, H. J. (2000). Structural flaws in the bridge from basic research on marriage to interventions for couples. *Journal of Marriage and the Family, 62*, 256–264.

Stewart, A. J., Copeland, A. P., Chester, N. L., Malley, J. E., & Barenbaum, N. B. (1997). *Separating together: How divorce transforms families*. New York: Guilford Press.

Stewart, S. D. (1999). Nonresident mothers' and fathers' social contact with children. *Journal of Marriage and the Family, 61*, 894–907.

Stewart, S. D., Manning, W. D., & Smock, P. J. (2003). Union formation among men in the U.S.: Does having prior children matter? *Journal of Marriage and Family, 65*, 90–104.

Strohschein, L. (2005). Parental divorce and child mental health trajectories. *Journal of Marriage and Family, 67*, 1286–1300.

Stroup, A. L., & Pollock, G. E. (1999). Economic consequences of marital dissolution for Hispanics. *Journal of Divorce and Remarriage, 30*, 149–166.

Sun, Y. (2001). Family environment and adolescents' well-being before and after parents' marital disruption: A longitudinal analysis. *Journal of Marriage and Family, 63*, 697–713.

Sun, Y., & Li, Y. (2001). Marital disruption, parental investment, and children's academic achievement: A prospective analysis. *Journal of Family Issues, 22*, 27–62.

Sun, Y., & Li, Y. (2002). Children's well-being during parents' marital disruption process: A pooled time-series analysis. *Journal of Marriage and Family, 64*, 472–488.

Sun, Y., & Li, Y. (2007). Racial and ethnic differences in experiencing parents' marital disruption during late adolescence. *Journal of Marriage and Family, 69*, 742–762.

Sun, Y., & Li, Y. (2008). Stable postdivorce family structures during late adolescence and socioeconomic consequences in adulthood. *Journal of Marriage and Family, 70*, 129–143.

Tashiro, T., & Frazier, P. (2003). "I'll never be in a relationship like that again": Personal growth following relationship breakups. *Personal Relationships, 10*, 113–128.

Tashiro, T., Frazier, P., & Berman, M. (2006). Stress-related growth following divorce and relationship dissolution. In M. A. Fine & J. H. Harvey (Eds.), *Handbook of divorce and relationship dissolution* (pp. 361–384). Mahwah, NJ: Lawrence Erlbaum.

Teachman, J. (2000). Diversity of family structure: Economic and social influences. In D. H. Demo, K. R. Allen, & M. A. Fine (Eds.), *Handbook of family diversity* (pp. 32–58). New York: Oxford University Press.

Teachman, J. D. (2002). Childhood living arrangements and the intergenerational transmission of divorce. *Journal of Marriage and Family, 64*, 717–729.

Teachman, J. D. (2003). Premarital sex, premarital cohabitation, and the risk of subsequent marital dissolution among women. *Journal of Marriage and Family, 65*, 444–456.

Teachman, J. D. (2008). Complex life course patterns and the risk of divorce in second marriages. *Journal of Marriage and Family, 70*, 294–305.

Teachman, J. D., Tedrow, L. M., & Crowder, K. D. (2000). The changing demography of America's families. *Journal of Marriage and the Family, 62*, 1234–1246.

Teachman, J., Tedrow, L., & Hall, M. (2006). The demographic future of divorce and dissolution. In M. A. Fine & J. H. Harvey (Eds.), *Handbook of divorce and relationship dissolution* (pp. 59–82). Mahwah, NJ: Lawrence Erlbaum.

Terhell, E. L., Broese van Groenou, M. I., & van Tilburg, T. (2004). Network dynamics in the long-term period after divorce. *Journal of Social and Personal Relationships, 21*, 719–738.

Thomas, C. E., Booth-Butterfield, M., & Booth-Butterfield, S. (1995). Perceptions of deception, divorce disclosures, and communication satisfaction with parents. *Western Journal of Communication, 59*, 228–245.

Thornton, A., & Young-DeMarco, L. (2001). Four decades of trends in attitudes toward family issues in the United States: The 1960s through the 1990s. *Journal of Marriage and Family, 63,* 1009–1037.

Thuen, F., & Eikeland, O. J. (1998). Social support among males and females after marital disruption. *Psychology, Health, and Medicine, 3,* 315–326.

Thuen, F., & Rice, J. (2006). Psychological adaptation after marital disruption: The effects of optimism and perceived control. *Scandinavian Journal of Psychology, 47,* 121–128.

Tucker, M. B., & Mitchell-Kernan, C. (1995). Social structural and psychological correlates of interethnic dating. *Journal of Social and Personal Relationships, 12,* 341–361.

Uebelacker, L. A., Courtnage, E. S., & Whisman, M. A. (2003). Correlates of depression and marital satisfaction: Perceptions of marital communication style. *Journal of Social and Personal Relationships, 20,* 757–769.

Umaña-Taylor, A. J., & Alfaro, E. C. (2006). Divorce and relationship dissolution among Latino populations in the United States. In M. A. Fine & J. H. Harvey (Eds.), *Handbook of divorce and relationship dissolution* (pp. 515–530). Mahwah, NJ: Lawrence Erlbaum.

Umberson, D., & Williams, C. L. (1993). Divorced fathers: Parental role strain and psychological distress. *Journal of Family Issues, 14,* 378–400.

Upchurch, D. M., Aneshensel, C. S., Sucoff, C. A., & Levy-Storms, L. (1999). Neighborhood and family contexts of adolescent sexual activity. *Journal of Marriage and the Family, 61,* 920–933.

U.S. Census Bureau. (2007). Survey of income and program participation, 2004 panel, wave 2 topical module, table 6. Retrieved at http://www.census.gov/population/www/socdemo/marr-div/2004detailed_tables.html

U.S. Census Bureau. (2008). *Families and living arrangements: 2007.* Washington, DC: Government Printing Office.

U.S. National Institute of Justice. (2000). *Extent, nature, and consequences of intimate partner violence* (No. NCJ 181867). Washington, DC: Office of Justice Programs and National Institute of Justice.

Vaillant, C. O., & Vaillant, G. E. (1993). Is the U-shaped curve of marital satisfaction an illusion? A 40-year study of marriage. *Journal of Marriage and the Family, 55,* 230–239.

Vangelisti, A. L. (2006). Hurtful interactions and the dissolution of intimacy. In M. A. Fine & J. H. Harvey (Eds.), *Handbook of divorce and relationship dissolution* (pp. 133–152). Mahwah, NJ: Lawrence Erlbaum.

Vannoy, D. (2000). Roles in the divorce process and identity strength. *Journal of Divorce and Remarriage, 32,* 101–118.

Videon, T. M. (2002). The effects of parent–adolescent relationships and parental separation on adolescent well-being. *Journal of Marriage and Family, 64,* 489–503.

Vlosky, D. A., & Monroe, P. A. (2002). The effective dates of no-fault divorce laws in the 50 states. *Family Relations, 51,* 317–324.

Wallerstein, J. S., & Kelly, J. B. (1980). *Surviving the breakup: How children and parents cope with divorce.* New York: Basic Books.

Walzer, S. (2008). Redoing gender through divorce. *Journal of Social and Personal Relationships, 25,* 5–21.

Walzer, S., & Oles, T. P. (2003). Accounting for divorce: Gender and uncoupling narratives. *Qualitative Sociology, 26,* 331–349.

Wang, H., & Amato, P. R. (2000). Predictors of divorce adjustment: Stressors, resources, and definitions. *Journal of Marriage and the Family, 62,* 655–668.

Weinberg, H., & McCarthy, J. (1993). Separation and reconciliation in American marriages. *Journal of Divorce and Remarriage, 20,* 21–42.

Westberg, H., Nelson, T. S., & Piercy, K. W. (2002). Disclosure of divorce plans to children: What the children have to say. *Contemporary Family Theory, 24,* 525–542.

Wheaton, B. (1990). Life transitions, role histories and mental health. *American Sociological Review, 55,* 209–223.

Whitehead, B. D. (1993, April). Dan Quayle was right. *The Atlantic Monthly,* 47–84.

Willén, H., & Montgomery, H. (2006). From marital distress to divorce: The creation of new identities for the spouses. *Journal of Divorce and Remarriage, 45,* 125–147.

Williams, D. R., Takeuchi, D. T., & Adair, R. K. (1992). Marital status and psychiatric disorders among Blacks and Whites. *Journal of Health and Social Behavior, 33,* 140–157.

Wojtkiewicz, R. A. (1992). Diversity in experiences of parental structure during childhood and adolescence. *Demography, 29,* 59–68.

Wolfinger, N. H. (2005). *Understanding the divorce cycle.* New York: Cambridge University Press.

Wu, L. L., & Martinson, B. C. (1993). Family structure and the risk of a premarital birth. *American Sociological Review, 58,* 210–232.

Wu, L. L., & Thomson, E. (2001). Race differences in family experience and early sexual initiation: Dynamic models of family structure and family change. *Journal of Marriage and Family, 63,* 682–696.

Xu, X., Hudspeth, C. D., & Bartkowski, J. P. (2006). The role of cohabitation in remarriage. *Journal of Marriage and the Family, 68,* 261–274.

Author Index

Subject Index

Academic achievement of
  children, 125–126
Account-making:
  as divorce recovery tool, 106
  postdivorce, 24–25
  See also Narratives
Adultery, as grounds for divorce, 61
African Americans:
  adjustment to divorce and, 20
  divorce and, 59–60
  divorce rates and, 77
  women, and the sociohistorical
    context, 19
  See also Race
Age:
  as cross-cultural context
    of divorce, 60
  variations in children's, 133–134
Aggression:
  marital, 80–81
  psychological and physical, 76
  See also Violence
Alcohol abuse:
  race and, 112
  See also Substance abuse
Alimony. *See* Spousal maintenance
American Law Institute (ALI), 64
Angry associates, as coparenting
  style, 120
ANOVAs/MANOVAs, analyses
  of, 41, 45

Behavioral mediators, 81
Behavioral observation, 40

Behavioral problems, children and:
  in multiple family transitions,
    142–145
  postdivorce, 128
  postdivorce, with married
    parents, 135
Behavior Problems Index, 129
"Best interest of the child"
  standard, 66–68
Bioecologial systems
  theory, 18–19
Blended families, challenges of
  children in, 6
Boys. *See* Gender

Child custody, 65–69
Children:
  decrease in economic
    resources and, 32
  effects of joint custody on, 8–9
  experiences and outcomes
    of, in divorce, 4–7
  involvement in separation
    process, 101–103
  multiple family transitions
    and, 35, 137–147
  parenting and, during
    predivorce period, 14
  postdisruption adjustment and, 23–25
  predisruption adjustment and, 20–21
  protective factors and, 22
  single-parent homes and, 7–8
  transitions in living
    arrangements for, 7

About the Authors

David H. Demo is a Professor and Director of Graduate Studies in the Department of Human Development and Family Studies at the University of North Carolina at Greensboro. His research focuses on divorce and family transitions, changes in family relationships accompanying divorce, and the consequences of family transitions for family members' well-being. He has published widely in professional journals, and he has authored or coauthored numerous chapters in edited volumes. He has also authored or edited several books, including, the *Handbook of Family Diversity* (with Katherine R. Allen and Mark A. Fine), *Parents and Adolescents in Changing Families* (with Anne Marie Ambert), and *Family Diversity and Well-Being* (with Alan C. Acock), which received the Choice Magazine Outstanding Book Award. He has served on the editorial boards of several journals, and in 2007, he began a term as the editor of *Journal of Marriage and Family*. He is a Fellow of the National Council on Family Relations.

Mark A. Fine is a Professor in the Department of Human Development and Family Studies at the University of Missouri. He was the editor of *Family Relations* from 1993 to 1996 and was the editor of the *Journal of Social and Personal Relationships* from 1999 to 2004. His research interests lie in the areas of family transitions, such as divorce and remarriage; early intervention program evaluation; social cognition; and relationship stability. He was coeditor, along with David Demo and Katherine Allen, of the *Handbook of Family Diversity*, published in 2000 by Oxford University Press. He coauthored, along with John Harvey, *Children of Divorce: Stories of Hope and Loss*, published in 2004 by Lawrence Erlbaum; coedited, with John Harvey, *The Handbook of Divorce and Relationship Dissolution*, published in 2005 by Lawrence Erlbaum; and coedited, with Jean Ispa and Kathy Thornburg, *Keepin' On: The Everyday Struggles of Young Families in Poverty*, published in 2006 by Brookes Publishing Company. He has published almost 200 peer-reviewed journal articles, book chapters, and books. In 2000, he was selected as a Fellow of the National Council on Family Relations. Dr. Fine is a licensed psychologist and maintains a small clinical practice.

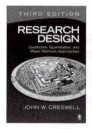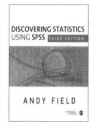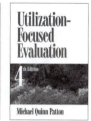